Producing Workshops, Seminars, and Short Courses

Producing Workshops, Seminars, and Short Courses
A Trainer's Handbook

John W. Loughary
Barrie Hopson

Association Press
Follett Publishing Company
Chicago

Library of Congress Cataloging In Publication Data

Loughary, John William, 1930–
   Producing workshops, seminars, and short courses.

   Includes index.
   1. Group work in education.   2. Forums (Discussion
and debate)   I. Hopson, Barrie, joint author.
II. Title.
LB1032.L69   371.3'7   79–11891
ISBN 0–695–81214–9

First Printing

Contents

Preface

This book is about doing short-term training. The idea for the book came from our shared observations that many workshops, seminars, and short courses are absolute disasters. Why should that be? Even though some kinds of learning are difficult, can't most instructional programs be at least interesting and in that sense enjoyable? Or are some topics simply dull by nature? We believe not—at least to the extent that you have some control over what you have agreed to teach, how you teach it, and the expectations and attitudes of your students. It also helps to have some program design, development, and evaluation skills.

One of the basic problems with short-term training is that people don't take it very seriously. People at times make some of the following assumptions:

If you can do it, you can teach it.

Teaching is simply telling and showing.

Everyone learns at about the same speed.

My subject is interesting to everyone.

Everyone wants to learn what I have to teach.

The simple truth is that these assumptions are often invalid.

Further, people selected to do short-term training may not be the best performers. The top salesperson is seldom selected to lead the training effort, nor is the best engineer, the most promising executive, or the successful manager. Usually less outstanding persons, who won't be missed if taken out of production, get the training nod. To make matters more difficult, they often are not trained for training others. If they happen to be perceptive and imaginative, have some natural smarts, and are motivated, they may do okay. But if they're not, the result can be training programs guaranteed to put the eagerest of beavers to sleep.

On the other hand, training programs can fail because people take them too seriously. Reading assignments are unrealistic, the limits of human attention spans are ignored, recreation is forbidden, and humor is viewed as disastrous as the plague.

In both instances—whether not taken seriously enough or taken too seriously—a short-term training program starts out with a handicap. When to that are added such conditions as poor student motivation, inferior facilities, and inexperienced instructors, it is no wonder that training is painful and unproductive.

Fortunately, there are means for avoiding some of these conditions, for compensating for those that are not avoidable, and for producing successful and interesting short-term training programs for any subject (at least any that we have encountered). Yes, there is an instructional technology.

It is this instructional technology that we will describe and illustrate in the following pages—but in a nontechnical manner.

Our intended audience consists of people who find themselves responsible for doing short-term training and who lack the experience and preparation for doing the job.

One way to think about the general concern of instruction is to identify four aspects: content—the substance of what you want people to learn; materials—the books, papers, films, and other things you use to assist learning and convey information; procedures—the actual behaviors you and your students do to learn the content; and climate—the physical and psychological environment in which it all takes place.

Our focus is on the last three aspects: materials, procedures, and climate. Our greatest emphasis will be on climate and procedures, in that order. These are largely independent of any particular content. Materials are more closely related to specific content, and so we treat them in a more general manner. We say nothing regarding content except as we provide examples from our own experiences. You must supply the content, and it can range from analyzing anagrams to zinging zithers.

Our purpose is to provide a basic model for producing short-term training programs and to illustrate how the model can be used. We contend that short-term training is different in some ways from traditional instruction. To maximize the usefulness of our model and suggestions, we want to share these differences with you. We do that in chapter 1. Chapter 2 develops the point of view that training is only one alternative for solving problems. As an alternative it should be compared with other solutions. Chapter 3 presents an overview of the five phases of the short-term training model. It provides brief descriptions and definitions of contracting, designing, developing, conducting, and evaluating short-term training. Following the overview, chapters 4 through 8 examine each phase of the model in detail. The final chapter consists of annotated references that we have found useful. They represent an initial introduction to the literature on instruction.

John W. Loughary
Barrie Hopson

Producing Workshops, Seminars, and Short Courses

1 The Nature of Short-term Training

FIVE DIMENSIONS OF SHORT-TERM TRAINING

Short-term training can mean different things to different people. It's a one-day orientation for new park rangers, a three-day carburetor repair school for mechanics, a one-week self-awareness laboratory for couples, a two-day legal briefing for legislators, a one-hour plant tour for new employees, a weekend communication workshop for families, a two-hour conference program on a new teaching technique, a four-week 747 jet school for pilots, a four-day financial planning course for preretirees, a four-hour chemical therapy seminar for physicians, a three-hour workshop for volunteer Sunday school teachers, a two-day women's consciousness-raising workshop, an eight-week technical procedure course for factory representatives, and a five-day communication skills workshop for supervisors.

Short-term training is all of these and more. It goes under a variety of names, including class, course, orientation, program, seminar, school, and workshop. Some call it training; others refer to it as education. Because it means different things to different people, it is important that we agree on a general definition.

Let's be as specific as possible. By short-term training we mean instruction that has the following characteristics:

1. It takes place within a period of one hour to three or four weeks.
2. It is a response to specific requests or problems.
3. Instructors and students alike are aware of the intensity in-

volved—the shortness of time for the amount and difficulty of what is to be learned.

Having noted these three characteristics of short-term training, we must say immediately that there are exceptions. From one perspective, any time you try to teach a subject in less time than what people believe is adequate or customary, you are doing short-term training. Thus a three-year bachelor's degree program could be viewed as short-term, as could a six-month master's degree program in engineering. At the other end of the scale, a thirty-minute orientation to company policies or a fifteen-minute "how to operate the widget maker" program could also qualify as short-term training.

However, in our search for a useful working definition of short-term training, we have settled on the one-hour-to-four-week time span—but acknowledge that there are exceptions.

It can be useful to view short-term training in terms of five dimensions: time, contractor, facilities, staff, and participants.

We've already discussed one dimension, that of time. The time dimension is often expressed via the intensity of short-term training. Short-term training is intense when you are attempting to teach much more than usual in a given period of time. It can also be intense when the lowest acceptable level of learning (performance) is very high. It can be intense because the learning goals are very specific. Time is probably the single most important dimension of short-term training. You have less of it than in traditional instruction. There is less flexibility, less room for error, and less opportunity for regrouping.

If, for example, you have sixty hours of instruction spread over twenty weeks, you can proceed at a relatively leisurely pace. When students have difficulty learning, there is sufficient time for corrective or remedial action. In contrast, when you are attempting to teach the same amount (sixty hours) in a two-week time period, it is a very different and usually more demanding situation. The impact of the time dimension will affect all other dimensions.

The second major dimension of short-term training is the contractor. Unlike much traditional instruction, which may be perpetuated without anyone's requesting it or questioning whether it should continue, most short-term training is initiated by someone other than the instructor. Whether you are working from within an organization, as an employee, or from without, as a consultant, someone has decided that training is the solution to a problem or concern and has requested you to solve it with a short-term training program. The problems you are asked to help solve can range from technical competence, to attitude change, to improving morale. In the vast majority of instances short-term training programs come into being with a purpose. The trainer, when accepting the responsibility to do the training, makes a contract with a contractor. The contractor dimension is important because it emphasizes that there are acknowledged expectations for the instruction and that an additional party to instructor and participants is interested in the outcomes of instruction. This differs from much traditional instruction, in which there is, in effect, no active contractor.

Facilities, the third dimension of short-term training, obviously are used by all training programs. The main issue regarding short-term training is that the facilities are often controlled and maintained by someone other than the trainer, and they may be very temporary. Consequently the instructor doing short-term training is often much less secure regarding adequacy and reliability of facilities than the instructor in a traditional setting.

Staff is the fourth dimension. In short-term training the instructional staff may have a high rate of change, resulting in relatively tentative working relationships. Procedures may be vague and personalities not well understood. Project staffs are often organized for a one-time-only program. Degree of commitment may be low or uncertain and accountability difficult to monitor. In other words, staff concerns are less structured and defined than they are in traditional instruction.

The fifth dimension of short-term training is participants. The basic issue, of course, is that they are students who are not students. Their primary role or occupation is something other than that of a full-time student. In fact, being a student for a short time is an interruption to their normal, regular life-style. It can be a pleasant interruption, but sometimes it is not. Participation in short-term training is sometimes mandated. Prerequisite skill levels may have been ignored. Conflicting status levels and inaccurate expectations may exist. The participant dimension obviously exists in traditional instruction, where it can also cause problems. The bind in regard to short-term training is that there is often very little time to deal with these problems.

Thus, our contention is that short-term training involves special characteristics and conditions that provide the instructors with challenges that are different from those of traditional instruction. The differences are of both degree and kind, but they are significant. We believe that examining the five dimensions of short-term training will clarify the major challenges that short-term training instructors encounter. We lead you through that examination in the next section.

DIMENSION 1: TIME

Intensity

The most dramatic condition of the time dimension is the intensity that can develop in short-term training programs, particularly in programs that use full-day schedules. Instructors and participants feel that they are working against the clock. People become very much aware of the passage of time, and they place increasing value on it. Each moment counts, and some people become irritated with those who waste time with seemingly irrelevant questions and impatient with those who seem to be slow learners. As instruction progresses, one can assume that learner problems will increase. More people will become confused about some of the instruction. How much time should the instructor devote to ongoing testing and review? How much deviation from the schedule should there be? Or is deviation even possible? In our experiences, we've seen programs where no deviation was allowed and an approximate fail-dropout rate was expected. The underlying philosophy was that this was economically better than expanding the length (and thus cost) of the programs to increase the number of participants completing them.

When programs become intense, instructors and students can become preoccupied exclusively with doing the tasks and thereby fail to maintain a supportive learning climate. Intensity, in other words, can breed discontent, frustration, and poor morale, which in turn can result in lowered learning rates. One of our more important tasks in the following chapters will be to illustrate how to prevent intensity from having such negative impact on short-term training.

Pace

Related to the issue of intensity is the problem of pacing short-term training. How does one establish or maintain a rhythm? In concentrated programs of several consecutive days' duration, there may be few rest periods. It is especially important, then, to select and determine the programs' high points and control the building up and relaxing that precedes and follows them. There are critical problems of information overload—how much can be absorbed—and of achieving an effective balance of instructional procedures. Students can be overwhelmed by too many audio-visual presentations and turned off by overkill didactic presentations and never-ceasing group discussions. Through the purposeful use of different instructional procedures, you can create a pace that facilitates learning.

An additional pacing problem can develop in programs that include several periods of noninstruction. In a program held during three consecutive weekends, for example, how can the enthusiasm developed by the end of the first weekend be sustained during the intervening week? How can you continue to affect participants' learning and attitudes when you are out of contact with them? Home assignments and buddy systems are two procedures whereby you can accomplish this.

In brief, pacing can be as important as program content. We've seen programs that, when viewed piece by piece, seemed excellent, but they failed in regard to both student interest and learning. The problem in each case was inadequate pacing. Students were overwhelmed with excellent presentations and experiences, but little thought had been given to pacing the events to maximize learning.

Low error tolerance

Another aspect of the time dimension is the low tolerance for instructor error. Once a short-term training program begins, there is little time to correct errors or to redesign and redirect. In programs with intervening nonteaching periods, such as a series of weekends, there is obviously some flexibility. Even so, when full days of instruction are involved, regaining lost ground is difficult. This means that careful planning and accounting for as many varied circumstances as possible is important. Poor learning experiences can result in more than the waste of precious time. Consider a problem-solving exercise that is poorly done and resisted by students. Besides the time wasted, the instructor has probably lost credibility and rapport. In addition to redoing the instruction, he or she must use additional time to rebuild the relationship with the students.

Ongoing assessment

Related to low error tolerance is the concern for ongoing evaluation of instruction. Because time is so precious in short-term training, it is important to know as soon as possible how successful the training is. In traditional programs, such as those lasting ten to eighteen weeks, instructors often feel less urgency about evaluation. They may wait until after several class sessions before giving an examination. And these midterms are usually intended to assess student performance rather than program effectiveness. In other words, the instructor and students view the results of the examinations in terms of the students' learning. If the results are poor, both instructor and student usually assign the student the responsibility for improving. If the problem is actually poor instruction, the instructor may sense this several weeks into the course and perhaps revise the approach. Even if this isn't done, there is time for the poorly performing student to seek out alternative sources of help.

Neither of these solutions to poor learning is feasible in short-term training. Short-term training programs may be over before the instructor realizes something is amiss. Even when trouble is sensed early, there is little time in which to change. Similarly, a student seeking alternative learning assistance does so in what can be an impossible short time period.

In order to be of much value, therefore, program evaluation information should be available immediately following the start of a program and continue throughout its life. While a difficult task, ongoing evaluation is quite feasible. For example, a first goal in many programs is to determine whether participant resistance exists and then to evaluate efforts to deal with it. Through the effective use of small group exercises, resistance can usually be assessed in ten to fifteen minutes. There are also methods of dealing with it in short time periods and ways to measure your effectiveness.

Termination points

Because of the relatively small amount of total time in short-term training programs, it is beneficial to be very clear about time periods within the program.

If, for example, participants are to do written work from 10:00 to 10:30 and then during the following period to use what they have written, it is essential that writing time begin and stop as scheduled. In a five-hour workshop, for example, to allow the writing period to slip fifteen minutes until 10:45 uses 5 percent of the total time available. If your schedule is tight, the 5 percent may be impossible to regain.

Instructors new to short-term training often overlook the importance of terminating periods as scheduled. They usually discover, however, that the traditional instructional luxury of wandering through topics, making irrelevant asides, and editorializing on the headlines of the morning newspaper get them into trouble. Don't misunderstand. Short-term training can be exciting, stimulating, entertaining, and fun. It is just that in most instances time allocations must be respected rigorously.

Another aspect of the termination idea is in relation to contractor and staff. Instruction in traditional settings can go on forever from the perspective of staff and contractors (administrators and boards of education). Semesters start and stop, students move on and graduate, programs change, but slowly. There is no hurry. What doesn't get done today may get done tomorrow.

Short-term training is different. Workshops and seminars are frequently produced once, never to happen again. There is no repeat. From the contractor's position this means that results are expected as of the termination date. Instructional staff members also have a perspective different from that in traditional settings. Professional payoffs and personal satisfaction must come within a short time period. When a program is finished, it is largely forgotten—all attention is given to the next one to be produced.

Goal specificity

Regardless of what one teaches or the format one uses, effective instruction is enhanced by being specific about goals and objectives. In recent years there has been a great emphasis on performance objectives, which means describing educational goals in terms of performance or behavior that would demonstrate that the learner had attained the goal. While these objectives are sometimes pushed to the ridiculous, both instructor and student benefit from clearly stated goals. Because of the limited time in short-term training, being specific about goals is especially important. It reduces unrealistic expectations of participants and aids staff in not being overly ambitious. Goal specificity can also make an important contribution to program design. Specific goals provide a means of assessing the contribution and function of each learning/teaching activity in a program.

DIMENSION 2: CONTRACTOR

Specific expectations

For both in-house and external trainers one major difference between short-term and long-term training is that the short-term trainer is contracted to do a specific piece of work. You are not hired, for example, as is a college instructor, to do a number of tasks, including the teaching of some courses. You are contracted to run specific training programs. You will be judged as successful or otherwise depending upon how the program fares. If you are an in-house trainer, you may be evaluated by other criteria as well, but you will be assessed for each program you run.

The contract document

Because short-term training programs come and go, an actual

contract document of some kind is especially important as a source of stability and a point of reference for program evaluation. In traditional training, educational institutions themselves provide the stability. There is, in a word, tradition upon which to rely.

Much short-term training occurs in less predictable and more dynamic environments. It is produced to meet specific demands and then disappears until the demands reappear. It happens relatively quickly, and consequently it is important to create a tangible referent regarding its nature and purpose—a contract that can substitute for tradition.

DIMENSION 3: FACILITIES

Materials development

If your film projector breaks down during a short course, you may not get a second chance to show your film. That's one difference between short- and long-term training. The quality of your materials must be higher, since you have no time to make up for inadequacies. Trainers spend considerable time developing punchy handouts and relevant slide shows, using films and videos only if they are central to the training objectives. Often materials are developed for one course's special needs and either cannot be reused or require revamping before being used with a different group. Another consideration is that materials must be prepared in advance. There is rarely an opportunity to produce materials once the course has begun.

Physical facilities

Climate building has to be done very quickly, and you need all the help you can get. For example, having an attractive building with good-sized rooms and adequate seating, lighting, and heating builds good climate. Unpalatable food and undrinkable coffee are irritants you can do without. It is vital that all the teaching materials and equipment you require are there and working. All of this has to be at the forefront of your mind in addition to the actual task of teaching the course. This is one reason why short-term training is often so stressful for trainers.

If anything goes wrong, you have to take time to make changes and rearrange the program. If you have a brilliant idea midway through the course, you may have no opportunity or secretarial facilities to implement it.

Dependence on others

We went to a course as participants once when it was pouring rain. There was no shelter outside the building. We had to wait until the trainer arrived, and he in turn had to find the janitor to let us in. It helps to have a better start than that! Great courses require good relationships between trainers, but equally important is the cooperation of everyone else involved in any part of the program.

You are often dependent upon others to provide technical equipment and materials. Technicians, perhaps above all others, are to be treasured. Even if you have the expertise, you yourself will probably not have the time to make necessary repairs.

At times, you have to be pleasant and warm to people who appear to be walking icebergs. There's no time to try to change them and no advantage in your being unpleasant. You could cheerfully strangle them, but you need them. That's yet one more strain for the trainers to grin and bear!

DIMENSION 4: STAFF

Planning for staff relationships

In a long-term course you can allow staff relationships to develop gradually. Difficulties can be ironed out over a period of time when the right moment occurs. With short-term training the right moment is before the course ever starts. Staff problems are likely to affect the course and will be played out in front of the participants. It is usually difficult to isolate yourself from a fellow trainer with whom you have problems, as might be possible in a school or college setting. In addition, how the staff behave is one of the strongest motivators for getting trainee participation. You are important role models.

Planning skills requirements

If a successful trainer needs above all else to be superhuman, he or she also needs to be part computer. A trainer has to be able to think sequentially and always in terms of alternatives: "If we put a lecture in there, we had better follow it with something active—an exercise or role play." A trainer also has to think constantly in terms of time: "It will take five minutes to demonstrate the skill; we'll put the participants into pairs, and that will take two to three minutes. They will then need to find space for themselves and notebooks and pencils—say, five minutes altogether. We have thirty minutes before coffee; so they could have five minutes' practice, five minutes' feedback, reverse, which leaves ten minutes for a large group session." A trainer also needs to be on the ball at mental arithmetic: "Here are twenty-seven trainees; but we don't want more than five in each group, and that is six groups, three of five and three of four."

A trainer has to be meticulous over detail without becoming obsessive. He or she has developed checklists—mental and actual—that enable him or her to proceed through contracting, choosing teaching procedures, organizing physical facilities, planning meals, and developing key relationships. A trainer has to anticipate problems, build in fail-safe procedures, and plan for equipment failures.

All teachers should think in terms of outcomes, alternative strategies, choosing between teaching alternatives and practices, simultaneously assessing effects on the learning climate, monitoring the event, concentrating on student needs. But if a short-term trainer does not do so, disaster is courted. Unlike for long-term courses, a trainer will probably get only one chance.

Leadership sensitivity to participants

Because success is a consequence of a good learning climate, the trainer needs to be extra sensitive to how participants are reacting. What do they look like when they arrive? Which of their moods are likely to be baggage brought in from elsewhere, and which are a result of the course? Participant reactions need constant monitoring. Should you slow down, build in a rest pause, tell a funny anecdote, get them to do something active to inject some energy, ask for feedback, check expectations? In short-term training, relationships have to be developed quickly. Staff cannot wait for a "natural" progression to occur. Nature has to be hurried along a bit. Climates can happen, or you plan for them to happen. In short-term training you have no alternative but to plan for them to happen.

The trainer notes the verbal behavior of the participants—what does he or she really mean when saying that there isn't time to complete the homework assignment? You become adept at reading nonverbal behavior—doodling, nervous finger tapping, staring vacantly, rushing to get out, sudden silence when you approach.

You never stop monitoring. Some of the most useful data you receive will come in the more relaxed atmosphere of coffee and meal breaks.

Range of teaching procedures

You need a greater range of procedures and structures than most traditional teachers typically employ. Short-term training is not simply giving a set spiel in the hope that many participants will be able to make some sense of it. Every input requires planning. Every session is designed in terms of what has come before and what might come after.

You need to be aware of new teaching techniques, materials, and training technology. Innovation and experimentation are two of your survival skills. You have to be able to think on your feet, turning reactions, even negative ones, into usable data. Participants' responses are often unpredictable, and you need a variety of alternative strategies to cope with them.

Instant credibility

If you have a group for only a day, you have to gain their confidence immediately. There is not time for the gradual buildup of trust and respect. You have to become an expert in the ways of establishing credibility—precourse literature, which just happens to mention your achievements, mid-course anecdotes that convey the range of your experiences.

The key to instant credibility, of course, is not name- or success-dropping but the ability to demonstrate your competence through course arrangements and precourse publicity, being clear in your objectives at the beginning, showing concern and flexibility by on-course contract building with participants, having a reason for everything that you are doing and asking of them, having equipment that works and enough well-organized and concise handouts to go around, being sociable, listening, being open, sharing appropriate aspects of yourself, and being aware of feelings and using them constructively.

Participants have to develop confidence in you so that they will be prepared to risk themselves or at least give you the benefit of the doubt and go along with the program. The first thirty minutes are vital, the first five minutes crucial. Do you convey warmth? Do you demonstrate that all contributions are valued? How do you deal with the first negative reaction? Sometimes you are quite clearly being tested. Are you prepared for it?

Staff's physical and mental health

Short-term training is the most demanding and exhausting teaching work we know. The payoffs can be high. The costs can sometimes be too high. We know independent full-time trainers whose life-styles involve long periods away from home, considerable traveling, too much food and drink, not enough sleep and recreation. Marriage casualties are high; friendships are often instant. (This is, of course, an extreme, but part-time and in-house trainers are subject to some of the same pressures.)

DIMENSION 5: PARTICIPANTS

In many ways participants in short-term training programs present the same kinds of problems and concerns as traditional students. After all, people are people. Nevertheless, people within the context of short-term training programs can present relatively unique concerns to instructors. These concerns are all related to the premium placed on time.

Resistance

Nothing can be as devastating to short-term training programs as participant resistance. Resistance occurs when, for whatever reason, there is opposition to participating in the planned program of instruction. Resistance also occurs in traditional instructional programs, but the longer time span and less intense pace usually allow more time to overcome or eliminate it. Even though very frustrating, resistance can be seen as an understandable reaction once its sources are understood. Resistance can develop for many reasons, including forced or involuntary attendance, difficult learning tasks, personally threatening learning situations, lack of interest in topics, lack of challenge, personality clash, and dislike of the learning procedure used.

Whatever the source of resistance, participants who want to oppose your program will usually have no trouble finding fault with you, your methods and materials, the facilities, the schedule—almost any part of your program. That is true because resistance is not necessarily rational. Very often it is not. People begin with the thought "I don't want to participate in the program," then quickly translate that into "I should not have to participate in this program." Then that thought is expanded to "This program is poorly done—so I have every right to resist it."

Climate building

Whether or not resistance exists, the building of an effective learning climate is a basic consideration of short-term training. We believe that it is often the paramount concern. A positive, supporting, and encouraging learning climate can compensate for many kinds of program shortcomings. In other words, within a healthy learning climate, people can learn in spite of a poor program.

What is a learning climate? There is no single set of specifications, but there are certain basic characteristics regardless of the specific form. First is that participants feel accepted and respected. They may be nervous, anxious, and uncertain, but in a healthy climate the instructor has communicated his or her respect and concern to the participants. In order to develop such an awareness, the instructor needs a genuine respect for individual differences. He or she must understand that not everyone will find the subject exciting, that some people may have difficulty learning it, and that people have different learning styles. When instructors don't have this awareness and acceptance of individual differences in values, interests, and abilities, they can quickly and effectively offend and put down students. A negative and hostile climate can soon develop in which some students, in addition to attempting to learn the subject matter, are also dealing with defensive and negative emotions.

People don't respond well to people whom they dislike, distrust, or resent. In traditional instruction there is often sufficient time to search out resources (other students, books, journals) and learn in spite of a negative learning climate. In short-term training there are no such alternatives. Participants' perceptions of the instructor are the main determinant of climate, and the instructor's behavior largely determines that perception.

Checking participant expectations

Participants arrive at training programs with some kind of "set" regarding what is likely to take place and what is to be gained from the forthcoming experience. Their expectations may range from very specific to none. But they will have some mental set.

It is important for you to assess their expectations very soon. If, for example, you intend to teach human relations skills, and they come expecting to learn techniques for increasing sales volume, then the sooner you—and they—discover the discrepancy, the better. Assessing participant expectations and sharpening your contract with them is a very good means of assuring effective instruction/learning. Not to do so is often self-defeating. This, incidentally, involves more than informing participants about your goals. It is not uncommon to see instructors state their objectives and never check to see if they are consistent with student expectations. The attitude of "You can like it or lump it" may be possible in a traditional instruction setting, but it is usually disastrous in short-term training. While there can be a good reason for an instructor's not changing a course to meet student expectations, an unwillingness to discuss expectation discrepancies suggests a defensive and insecure instructor.

Follow-up/applications

Another participant consideration that differentiates much short-term from traditional training is follow-up concerns. Because so much short-term training has specific purposes and immediate applications, participants want to use what they have learned. Their friends, colleagues, and families may see them as having made significant changes in their thinking, feeling, and behaving. These associates, however, may not be ready for the changes. The literature is full of stories about people returning from two-week sensitivity training programs full of love and openness, only to encounter criticism and rejection. They changed, but the rest of their worlds remained the same. This issue extends to a broader range of concerns than sensitivity training. People learning new management and supervisory procedures, new accounting methods, new eating habits, and new ways of solving problems are examples of short-term training participants who may encounter opposition when they apply their new learning in old situations. Almost anything one learns that results in different behavior can receive negative reactions from others. If the reactions are sufficiently strong, the participant may react by stopping the new behavior, particularly if he or she is the only person in the group who attended the training program.

In training jargon, the problem is lack of reinforcement of the new behavior after returning home. The problem can exist even without negative reactions. One of the first things participants may discover upon trying the new behavior is that they don't understand it as well as they thought they did. The procedure for resolving family squabbles or the system for scheduling supplies seemed very clear on the last day of the course. But now certain ideas and details are fuzzy. To whom can participants turn for follow-up information? And where can they receive reinforcement for continuing to apply the new skills and procedures until they are perfected?

LOOKING AHEAD

That, then, is the nature of short-term training. We have discussed several ways in which it differs from traditional instruction. In chapter 3 a five-phase model for producing short-term training programs is described. Chapters 4 through 8 are devoted to further descriptions and illustrations of how the model can be used. Even though we describe the five steps in sequence, it is clear that many training programs are not developed that systematically. One moves back and forth from one phase to another until requirements are worked out and issues become clear. It should be helpful, nevertheless, for purposes of understanding the model, to begin with an overview. This is presented in the next chapter.

2 Solving Problems Through Training

ALTERNATIVE SOLUTIONS

When organizations face problems involving people, training is nearly always seen as a possible solution. In one way or another the problem involves getting people to change their behavior or attitudes, and a logical method for doing that is training. There are other methods for solving problems, and it is wise to consider them before assuming that training is the solution.

If we agree that a problem is a discrepancy between existing and desired conditions, then there are at least three ways of reducing the discrepancy. These are as follows:

1. Training people: those involved learn new behaviors, concepts, and attitudes and change ones that exist.
2. Changing environmental conditions: rearrange materials and equipment, relocate, acquire different systems, change personnel.
3. Redefining values: change expectations, goals, policies, or priorities so that existing conditions fall within tolerances.

Training is not always the best solution. And, obviously, many problems are solved best by a combination of the three methods. Thus the critical first step for you as a short-term trainer is to determine the extent to which training can contribute to resolving the discrepancy (problem) in question.

Consider the following illustration.

Mr. and Mrs. Tom Swift started Swift Travel as a couple. They now have six employees. This sounds like success, except that with the addition of each employee, the Swifts' profit rate decreased. A problem now exists. It is the discrepancy between existing costs of doing business and the desired costs. It is clear that the Swifts have a problem. The Swifts may believe that the employees have a problem: There is a discrepancy between their existing level of efficiency and the desired level. But whose desired level? The employees may be very content with existing conditions. What about the Swifts' customers? Are they content? Apparently. On the other hand, would they continue to be satisfied if the Swifts changed customer services?

While training may at first seem the obvious means of resolving the discrepancy between actual and desired staff performance, the situation is really not that simple. Let's see how the problem at Swift Travel might be approached in terms of the three kinds of solutions.

1. Increase skills or ability. The Swifts might take a management supervision course, visit other agencies and observe how they operate, or institute a staff-training program.
2. Change the environmental conditions. They might reorganize assignments, decrease or increase staff, reduce frill services, lease a computer, purchase reference aids, or rearrange the office layout.
3. Redefine the problem. A fairly limited solution in this case. But they could decide that the decreased profit rate was, after all, acceptable.

Thus the Swifts have several alternative means of reducing their discrepancy. Training is only one.

EVALUATING THE TRAINING ALTERNATIVE

How does one decide whether or not to choose training as a

solution to a problem? One means we find useful is to ask the following questions:

1. What are the discrepancies that concern you or your client? Which of these are shared by other people?
2. Are there parts of the problem for which training seems a reasonable solution? Would increasing people's knowledge and ability help reduce the discrepancy between existing and desired conditions?
3. What are the training goals and desired outcomes? What are the information, behaviors, and attitudes you want to effect?
4. What nontraining alternative solutions could be used?
5. Is training economically and practically feasible as compared with the alternatives? Are people sufficiently motivated?

We can illustrate the procedure by applying the questions to the Swift Travel situation.

Describe the discrepancy

To repeat, the profit percentage rate has been going down as business volume and staff have increased. The Swifts believe that they can increase business volume, but they must do so without the cost of hiring more staff. The discrepancy in effect is between the results that the staff currently achieves and those that the Swifts desire them to achieve. A positive attitude exists. Staff members enjoy working at Swift Travel and would like to be more productive. They all believe that they are currently working hard.

Appropriateness of training

To answer this question, the Swifts paid special attention to observing the staff function. They also talked to several customers about the services they received. Finally, they followed several customer orders from beginning to end. Based on this information, they developed a list of problem points, which included the following:

• There were several important functions for which no one had specific responsibility, including desk and telephone reception. Everyone helped as the needs arose. Some employees were much more informed and effective than others, while some were not helpful.

- All supervision was done by the Swifts.

- All staff members did typing, but some were poor typists.

- The time required to plan trips with clients varied greatly among staff. Some of the staff had pleasant, effective routines, while others seemed to fumble through their sessions with customers.

- An expensive travel information filing system to which the Swifts subscribed was misused by all staff members.

- Customers reported staff to be pleasant but often uncertain and inefficient.

The Swifts explored their problem in depth. It is clear from this partial list that training is a reasonable solution to parts of their problem. Three major training problems appear to be (1) use of information resources, (2) trip-planning procedures and techniques, and (3) customer relations.

Training goals

The Swifts summarized the goals and listed them under the headings of Information, Behavior, and Attitude for each of their three training problems.

Problem: Use of Information Resources

Information   Understand scope of information included.
Explain filing and cross-filing methods used.
Grasp limits of system.
Know how system relates to other information, such as airline schedules and travel brochures.

Behavior   Ability to use the system to solve several kinds of travel problems.

Attitude	Confidence in the system.
	Belief that the system used is the most efficient one.
	Comfortable in using the system.

Problem: Trip-Planning Techniques

Information	Know purpose of interviewing customers.
	Understand interviewing procedures.
	Work out customer follow-up procedures.
	Know record-keeping procedures.
Behavior	Complete interviews in specified time.
	Maintain specified records.
	Transfer and accept customers from other staff.
Attitude	Confidence in the interview procedure.
	Belief that customer's valuable time shouldn't be wasted.
	Pride in serving customers efficiently.

Problem: Customer Relations

Information	Be aware of customer's perspective.
	Understand company policy regarding billing, refunds, and credit.
Behavior	Have pleasant phone voice and observe etiquette.
	Apply understandings to customer inquiries.
	Discern when to refer customer to Mr. or Mrs. Swift.
Attitude	Desire to please customers.
	Value in working as team with staff.

The list isn't complete, but it does illustrate the kind of information needed to develop a clear idea of the kind of training involved. Using the outcomes or goals categories of information, behavior, and attitude helps assure that all important goals are included. In the case of Swift Travel, for example, there would be little point in teaching the staff the information and behavior (skills) required to use the information system if they thought it was worthless and wouldn't utilize it.

Nontraining alternatives

Before firing up a training program, it is helpful to identify possible alternatives. These may be less expensive, seem more powerful, or in some other way be preferable to the training solution. The Swifts thought of several nontraining alternatives. These include the following:

- Replace one staff member with an office manager.

- Replace two staff members with three or four clerks.

- Reorganize the operation and develop several specialist positions.

- Hire an organizational development firm.

- Have a computer company do a systems study.

It is difficult to separate training completely from these alternatives. This is true of many problem-solving situations.

Economic feasibility of training

Is the cost of a training program warranted? Often this is a tough question. An answer may require considerable analyses of overall costs and availability of resources. (And factors such as staff morale and time should be considered.) In the case of Swift Travel, however, it was fairly apparent that a logical step was to train staff to use existing resources. Until existing people and information resources were more effectively used, various kinds of reorganization were less attractive. So the Swifts went with training.

In addition to the primary outcomes, a training program often has secondary benefits. For example, it is difficult to design a training program without also developing a clearer understanding of your problem. It forces us off a general perspective of the problem onto an eye-level, nuts-and-bolts, hands-on contact. In order to produce an effective training program, we must become specific about what is wrong. Doing that can be 50 percent of the solution in itself.

3 Short-term Training Model

So you've decided that a training program is the preferred solution to your problem, or at least to parts of it. How do you get from this decision to actually producing the program? This chapter provides one answer as it summarizes our short-term training model.

The model consists of the following phases: contracting, designing, developing, conducting, and evaluating. In this chapter we will discuss the functions included in each phase. Chapters 4 through 8 are devoted to specific illustrations of the five respective phases.

CONTRACTING

There is usually some kind of agreement between you and the person who has asked you to produce a short-term training program. We recommend that a contract be agreed upon and recorded. The decision to produce a program is sometimes made before negotiating a contract, and other times it is part of the actual negotiation. Sometimes there is little or no negotiation or even no preliminary discussion between the contractor and the producer, and other times there is a great deal. If you are a member of the firm, you may receive a memo requesting (ordering) you to "teach the salespeople how to use the new ordering system," in which case contracting may consist of reading the memo and arranging dates and times for the training session. At the other extreme, you may be outside an organization and be asked to produce a company-wide human relations training program. The negotiations can be extended and involved. They could even result in a decision not to produce a program.

The basic function of the contracting phase is to clarify the purpose and desired outcomes and work out the operational ground rules. Budget facilities, staff, desired outcomes, participants, and selection procedures are important topics for contracting. Contracting can take two basic approaches. One is to attempt to include all the details and decisions that can be anticipated. The other is to establish the rules and procedures for making decisions, leaving the actual decisions until later. Our preference is to include some of both but to emphasize agreeing upon a procedure for making decisions. Obviously, decisions regarding costs and number of participants usually need to be firm. But, for example, during contracting it is usually wiser to establish criteria for participation than to list actual participants. We once produced a supervision skills workshop for first-line supervisors. During contracting discussions, it became clear that one important issue was lack of communication between these supervisors and their managers. There was widespread apprehension about the managers' power and support. Were they watchdogs or helpers? The question had not been well articulated, let alone answered. In any event, we believed that it would be helpful for the supervisors to examine their relationships with the managers within the privacy of their (the supervisors) own group.

This point was accepted during our contracting discussions with the plant executive and had been conveyed only to the supervisors who were to participate, or so we assumed. We were surprised, then, when several managers appeared at the workshop and indicated that they were there to observe! Even giving them the benefit of the doubt regarding their intentions, the situation was unfortunate, for we had to deny their request. More to the point, the situation would also have been unnecessary had we made our concerns more explicit and checked our assumptions during the contract negotiations.

Another way of looking at contracting is to view it as the first step in building a healthy learning climate. It gives specific attention to basic decisions and decision-making criteria, which will be the foundation for everything else that is done. Confusion in the contract can foster confusion in the program. Unrealistic budgets promote unrealistic programs. Sloppy criteria and guidelines lead to controversial decisions. Unclear goals promote vague programs, and vague programs are difficult to evaluate.

At the completion of the contracting phase, you have a purpose, desired outcomes have been defined, and an agreement for producing a training program exists. In addition, you have given initial consideration to program content, instructional procedures, and learning climate.

DESIGNING

Designing a program is the process of describing what it should accomplish and how. It may be a simple list of topics and teaching procedures or a complex chart that describes how people, materials, and equipment will interact to produce the program's goals. A program design is akin to a plan or blueprint. It is the basis for developing the actual program. The designing phase includes several steps. The following are the most important:

- Becoming more specific about outcomes.

- Determining people, material, and equipment specifications.

- Sequencing activities.

A brief comment about each of these steps should be useful. Becoming more specific about outcomes involves applying values to the general outcomes developed during the contract negotiations—in other words, deciding how much and how well you want people to learn. This will vary from situation to situation. For example, if your objective is to teach people to conduct plant tours, you will probably demand a lower performance level than if you are training paramedics to use new lifesaving equipment.

If you are doing a short art or music appreciation course, is performance level even important? Probably not. Participant enjoyment is probably paramount. You will let them determine how much they want to learn from and enjoy the experience. Nevertheless, you still may want to become more specific about the ways in which participants can experience enjoyment—what payoffs besides competencies they are pursuing. Being specific about these provides a basis for designing a more satisfying course. You may have come to this level of specificity in the contracting phase, but if not, now is the time to sharpen program goals.

It is important to remember that the goal clarification does not end with the design phase. Working through the development and conducting phases can provide further insights into goals. While the benefits regarding goal clarification are by-products of the latter two phases, goal clarification per se is an essential aspect of designing programs.

The task of determining people, material, and equipment specifications consists basically of (1) deciding how course objectives are to be taught and (2) assuring a healthy learning climate. The task is one of considering instructional procedure alternatives, evaluating these in regard to such criteria as cost, time, and availability, and then selecting procedures to be used.

Note that the task is not to acquire people, material, or equipment but to describe the standards, qualities, or criteria that these must meet. Assume you are designing a short-term training program for instructing a group of physicians about the use of a new series of drugs. Since the program will be produced only once or twice, you decide not to build a media presentation but to use a live presenter instead. That is a design decision. The next decision, also part of design, is to list the criteria a live presenter must meet. You might come up with the following:

- Good voice delivery.
- Professional credentials—preferably M.D. or Ph.D.
- Technical familiarity with the related drugs.
- Professional credibility regarding experience or research.

Having listed your specifications, you then set about finding a speaker who meets them.

If you decide to include a thirty-five-millimeter slide presentation in a short-term training course for expectant parents, the following specifications for the presentation could be listed:

- Eighth-grade vocabulary level.

- Graphics instead of photos.

- Limit of six basic concepts.

- Definition of all technical terms prior to use.

- Avoidance of negative examples.

Add your content goals to the list, and you have a design from which a presentation can be developed.

Note that the specifications pay attention to both procedures and learning climate. It is important to think through both the procedures to be used to teach an objective and the context within which the procedure will be used.

The final aspect of the design phase is to sequence the various teaching/learning procedures. What will be taught first, second, and so on? When will reviews and tests come, if at all?

How should you mix media? A morning of lectures and an afternoon of movies? Deadly! Physical movement following meals is best. Instructor fatigue is another consideration. When the sequencing is done, then you have an initial schedule of events.

When the design phase is complete, you are clear about the developmental work that must be done in order to conduct the program.

DEVELOPING

This is the phase in which you put content and procedures together. It involves developing teaching materials, planning and rehearsing instructional procedures, making arrangements for equipment and facilities, checking the program for possible deterrents to climate, and making administrative arrangements (for example, rooms, meals, stipends, and expense checks).

These are the last activities before the short-term program is actually conducted. In the development phase, the design specifications on paper are translated into actual materials and real activities.

Depending upon the complexity of the particular short-term training program and your prior experience with the topic, the development phase can involve the testing of materials and procedures. For example, using a questionnaire that is unclear to participants or presenting confusing directions for a learning exercise has a negative effect on the usefulness of the learning procedures involved and also detracts from a healthy climate. Participants don't like to be confused. It can cause some to be defensive, and in turn they blame you for being incompetent. That is no way to build climate.

Another reason for testing materials and procedures is to determine whether they do what you intend them to do. A perfectly clear procedure may not have the desired result. We once brought a group of five- and six-year-old children into a workshop to demonstrate how easily they could learn some concepts via a gaming procedure. What actually took place was disastrous. The children didn't like the game and wouldn't cooperate, and the situation verged on chaos. We demonstrated just the opposite of what we had intended. It was clear as soon as the exercise was over, however, that making a few small adjustments in our instructions would have made it very effective. Testing the procedure prior to using it would have identified the needed adjustments.

Testing experiential learning activities in which participants risk their self-esteem is important, especially when you are not familiar with the values and assumptions of your participants. Instructors who move from high school or university teaching to adult education settings are often surprised when procedures and materials they have developed don't work well in the adult setting. The issue is not better or poorer students but rather different values, assumptions, and expectations. For example, college students are more or less used to small group discussions. Thus, when they are told to break up into small discussion groups, they know the routine. When, in contrast, you ask a class of shipping clerks to break up into groups of four and identify points of the presentation that are confusing, chances are that you will not achieve the desired results. The participants, having few or no small group behavior skills, may be very self-conscious and thus sit staring at their feet. In this example, testing your procedure (presentation, small group discussion, and question/answer session) might consist simply of thinking through what you are requesting them to do and considering whether it is a reasonable request, given their experience. If it seems questionable, then you might prepare a list of discussion questions to guide their small group work. When the development phase is completed, you are ready to conduct your program.

CONDUCTING

This phase involves the actual presenting of the short-term training program. It may begin with the first contact with participants as they arrive or, in more complex programs, with prearrival work. Examples of the latter would be a first on-site staff meeting or setting up equipment prior to the opening session.

In regard to climate, the first contact with participants is especially important. They should feel expected, welcome, and, as quickly as possible, part of the assembled group. Twenty minutes devoted to ice-breaking or warm-up activities can establish a group cohesiveness and a readiness to participate that can require days to develop when participants' personal concerns are ignored. Many times cohesiveness in training programs never occurs, and some participants leave courses feeling more uncomfortable than when they arrived.

Participants who are preoccupied with their own discomfort and anxiety are less able to focus on the task of the course. It is puzzling why some instructors from traditionally oriented settings don't recognize this. In our workshops on teaching procedures, we have often raised the issue. Some instructors participating in these classes respond that they really aren't concerned with how the students feel. The students are there to learn, and the instructors are there to teach. They simply want to get on with teaching.

This is a bit like arranging for a vacation at a nudist camp with one's friend without first assessing his or her attitudes regarding nudity.

Admittedly, some instructors have a natural way of putting people at ease—whether the people are participants in their courses or guests in their homes. But there are procedures that any instructor can use at the beginning of a course to make participants feel positive about being there. For example, given a group of complete strangers, it is possible in fifteen minutes to have each person know two or three others at more than just a surface level.

Conducting the workshop involves more than interacting with participants. Failure to attend to facilities and key staff when you are doing the course away from home can make or break a program. Janitors who must unlock doors and move equipment, secretaries who may be asked to make unanticipated arrangements and type or duplicate newly inspired materials, and cooks who are expected to serve meals on a tight schedule all need tending to.

Instructor credibility is another critical concern in conducting short-term training programs. There is insufficient time for developing it slowly. It must be established quickly. But honest attempts to establish instructor credibility can backfire and put you in a negative light. Name or place dropping is a classical example of a high risk attempt to establish credibility. Some participants will never have heard of Henry Wellknown; others will have but won't be impressed—Henry being a phony in their opinion; and a few will resent your using the "credibility by association" method. There are things that you can do, however. Have staff members introduce themselves and merge your self-introduction with the self-introductions of participants. Immediate demonstrations of competency and sensitivity to participant interests are other effective means of establishing your credibility.

Staff relationships are important and need tending. Providing evaluative feedback and reinforcement and making opportunities for debriefing and private time are examples of important staff concerns. We experienced an interesting situation in one workshop in which the staff had come to depend upon the leader for reinforcement and direction. For whatever reason, the leader was not his usual reinforcing, dynamic self during this short-term training program. Rather than complain and become upset, the other staff members agreed that the leader wasn't to be depended upon to serve his usual function and agreed to share it among themselves. Instead of wallowing in resentment and disappointment, they took responsibility for staff well-being.

Another important concern during the conducting phase is the implementation of alternative procedures. If the planned approach isn't working, what else can you do? Many short-term training instructors have had the experience of staying up half the night making major revisions after the first day of a workshop. This may be due to a bad contract or designing a program greatly at odds with the participants' expectations. Alternatives are also useful on a more immediate basis. Changing part of an exercise, reversing the sequence of presentation, and abandoning a prepared transparency for a freehand drawing on the chalkboard are examples. A real test of an instructor's competency regarding the conducting stage of short-term training is the ability to create alternatives on the spot. "Thinking on your feet," some people call it.

EVALUATING

Evaluation is the fifth and final phase of the short-term training model. Actually, some evaluation is done during the conducting phase. To the extent that you are collecting information and making judgments about the effectiveness of your training, you are evaluating. Clearly, in some training programs, evaluation begins almost immediately. To cite a simple example, one workshop we planned required as much time as we could squeeze out of the four eight-hour days available to us. To gain an extra thirty to forty minutes each day, we planned for morning and afternoon refreshments to be served during working sessions instead of taking the traditional coffee breaks. Anticipating possible opposition to this change from tradition, we observed reactions to the procedure during the first day and surveyed the group at the end of the day. The information we collected indicated clearly that our procedure was very unpopular and affected climate. Consequently we decided to change the schedule and reinstate regular coffee breaks.

In general, doing some kind of data collection and evaluation at the end of each major component of a short-term training program is useful. When pace and intensity are demanding, a small trouble can turn into a big problem. For example, a group of counselors were attending a workshop on the elements of psychological testing. By the beginning of the second day, the instructor felt he was losing about one-third of the group. He guessed that he had not been clear enough in his initial presentation and so repeated much of the material. Students still seemed to flounder, and by the end of the second day, he had blown his schedule seriously. A colleague, to whom he complained of his seeming failure, suggested testing the group—not on the material he had presented but on the four basic arithmetical functions. To make the story short, he did and discovered that one-third of the class could not do long division. Without that skill, it was impossible to learn much of what he was attempting to teach. Had he collected relevant information early in the program, he could have avoided what developed into a major problem.

We have referred to both collecting information and making judgments. Both are part of evaluation, and clearly distinguishing between them is important. When we collect information, we are trying to answer the question How many? How many learned the lesson? How many lessons did they learn? How many liked the teaching procedure? How many thought it was interesting? These are objective questions. We are, in a word, measuring the learning and attitudes of participants. Once we have that information, we can ask the How good? question. This is a subjective question. The answer depends on our values. There is nothing good or bad about the fact, for example, that participants learned 60 percent of the information presented. The judgment regarding whether that is adequate or not depends on other circumstances. If you are talking about a group that is being exposed to a complicated subject for the first time, or a group that does not really want to participate in your short-term training program, then 60 percent may not be half bad. It may, in fact, be very good. If, on the other hand, the short-term training program is a review session for people skilled in the subject, then a 60 percent rate may indicate trouble.

One of the common sources of problems in evaluating training. programs is making judgments without relevant information. An evaluation based on hunches and speculation is likely to be unduly influenced by wishful thinking and single dramatic events or atypical occurrences. Collecting information requires time and effort, but it is a necessary part of evaluation.

Evaluation of training usually has a double focus. One spotlight is on the outcomes of the program; it attempts to show participant achievement levels. How much did they learn? The second evaluation spotlight is on the teaching/learning process. This tries to clarify participants' reactions to the program. We find that trainers are generally less interested in the evaluation phase of short-term training than in other phases. When they do devote resources to evaluation, the focus is most likely to be on process rather than outcomes. One reason for this is the complexity of doing outcomes evaluation. It is often difficult to determine the extent to which participants achieved desired outcomes. Appraising their reaction to process, in contrast, involves little more than asking them.

This, in brief form, is the short-term training model.

Of course, it is rarely as neat as this in practice. You get to the development stage and realize that you do not have the go-ahead to approach particular trainers to join the staff, and you have to return to the contracting stage. You are conducting the workshop and discover with horror that a handout designed for a previous course has not been rewritten for the current course—instantly you are back to the development stage.

The main point is that the more aware you are of the five phases of short-term training production, the less likely it is that such problems will arise. The remainder of the book will examine each phase in detail to ensure that your chances of successful short-term training programs are maximized and that you enjoy running them, learn from each one, and live longer!

4 Contract Building

When a training course does not work, the postmortem more often than not indicates a malformed contract. For example, two trainers were asked by the training director of a large firm to train twenty employees as volunteer counselors in an alcohol and drug abuse program. The trainers had done some work with the company in years past and thus engaged in minimal negotiations regarding this program.

To their surprise, the course was a shambles. Of the twenty participants, three did not turn up until lunchtime on the first day. Others came and left for important appointments, thus totally disrupting the course, which was designed as a continuous learning experience.

What went wrong? The course was well designed, the trainers highly competent—so much so that the participants expressed genuine regret about not being able to attend, fully owing to previous arrangements.

The trainers had forgotten to remind the training director that full-time attendance was essential. They assumed that the director knew their courses well enough to realize that continuous attendance was essential. The design was such that each session required attendance at all previous sessions. The trainers' disastrous error had nothing to do with training per se but rather with contracting.

The road to training failures is paved with good assumptions.

CONTRACTS DEFINED

A contract is an agreement between two parties to do or not to do something for a specified consideration. A training contract between the trainer and the instructor should specify the follow-·ing points:

- training goals

- control issues—e.g., subcontracting of other staff, selection of participants

- budget

- dates and place of training

- evaluation issues—who does it, how, and when

- action plans

External trainers—those outside the organization—are used to thinking in terms of contracts, but internal trainers often are not. Yet, if anything, the danger of misunderstandings is often greater within an organization than between an organization and an external trainer. Here is an example. We accept a ludicrous request because we do not wish to offend a senior manager. We agree to run a weekend workshop on report writing simply because our bosses think it's a good thing. We know that the participants do not wish to attend; that they feel strongly that courses should be done on company time; and, furthermore, that they don't need a course in report writing. So we have a workshop, and it's a nonevent!

THE FUNCTIONS OF CONTRACTS

Because of legal overtones, some people are suspicious of contracts. "What do you mean, a contract? Don't you trust me?" A contract has less to do with trust and more to do with clarification. When people have to formulate a contract, it forces them to think through the issues—training goals may actually be specified! The contract provides a basis for a working relationship between trainer and contractor. It is clear evidence of a commitment on behalf of the contractor. And finally, it serves as a reference point to minimize future argument about what was to be done, who was to do it, and how much it was going to cost.

Some people express the concern that a contract limits one's flexibility. Too often this concern sounds like a request for a blank check. Are you really asking for flexibility—for if you are, this can be negotiated into the contract—or are you trying to hoodwink the contractor into something he or she might not choose if your intentions were really known? In the latter case you are heading for trouble.

KINDS OF CONTRACTS

The simplest form of contract is a verbal agreement. We are not recommending this, as it often allows the trainer and the contractor to avoid thinking through the issues. Sometimes a written memo summarizing a discussion might be all that is necessary. The following example shows what is usually covered in a written memo.

Worldwide Wonderful Widgets

6/6/79

MEMO

To: Gary Fenton
From: Joan Castle
Re: Training of Checkers

This confirms our agreement over lunch yesterday. The training department will put on three half-day courses to enable all your checkout personnel to be instructed in the checkout system coming into the store on September 1. They will be:
1. taught how to use the new machines.
2. shown how the data from the new machines will help in stock control.

The first course will be on July 8 in Room 212; the second on July 15 in Room 204; and the third on July 22 in Room 212.

A letter of agreement is sometimes drawn up.

Worldwide Wonderful Widgets

6/6/79

Dear Gary,

The training department will put on three three-hour courses for your department.

Objectives
1. To train all checkout personnel to use the new checkout machines that are to commence operation September 1.
2. To ensure a positive attitude toward the new system by demonstrating:
    a. that checkout staff can work faster, thereby assuring fewer disgruntled customers.
    b. how the machines collect data that will help with stock control, thereby simplifying jobs.
    c. that the new machines will not result in fewer jobs.

Place and Time
Course #1 July 8   9:00–12:00   Room 212
Course #2 July 15   9:00–12:00   Room 204
Course #3 July 22   9:00–12:00   Room 212

Equipment
Three of the new machines by July 1. Your department to arrange for this.

Staff Requirements
The training department has contracted the machine company and arranged for two of our staff to attend an orientation course on June 26 in Chicago. These two staff members can then plan our three courses.

Budget
Expenses for two staff members to attend
Chicago course $450
Training materials and manuals   90

Total $540

Evaluation

The course will have been a success if on the first day of full operation of the new machines (September 1), there is no more than one call for assistance from each member of the checkout staff.

One month later the checkout staff will be given a questionnaire to determine how positive they feel about the new system.

Would you please sign this agreement if you think that all points have been covered. If not, please contact me, and we will discuss the courses together. I need to know by June 12.

Yours sincerely,

Joan Castle
Training Manager

Signature of Agreement

_____
Gary Fenton

Date_____

This letter was drawn up after a discussion and contains points on which action is required as well as a summary of the requirements and responsibilities. A signed proposal would look similar to the letter of agreement except that it would be more tentative, usually being a response to a training problem that has been discussed generally by the contractor and the trainer.

At the other extreme of the contracting dimension from a verbal agreement is a legal contract. By definition, this will usually have been drawn up by lawyers or a legal department.

Trainer's Tip: Don't make assumptions about people's expectations. A good contract helps spell everything out and clarify your own thinking.

CONTRACTS AND IN-HOUSE TRAINING

Free-lance trainers by necessity have to develop contracting skills to make sure they eat. The degree of loose thinking that is often found in an organization wherein one department or individual agrees to put on a training course for another is remarkable.

An in-house trainer may not have the same freedom to reject a contract he or she is unhappy with as does a free-lance trainer, but the more aware the trainer is of the things that can go wrong, the more the likelihood of their happening can be minimized.

Trainer's Tip: A written contract is at least as important for in-house training as for external training.

THE CONTRACT TRIANGLE

Any training contract involves three parties: the contractor, the trainers, and the participants. Developing a contract involves three stages and produces a contract triangle as illustrated.

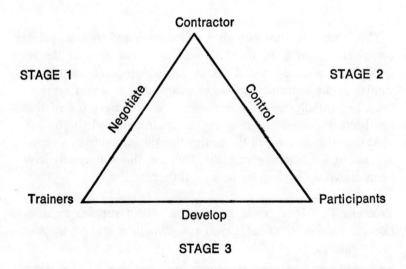

Stage 1: Between trainers and contractor

This stage always involves negotiation, usually culminating in a written agreement of some kind. Part of that agreement should center around trying to control what happens at Stage 2.

Stage 2: Between contractor and participants

Stage 2 involves trying to control what the contractor communicates to the participants. For example, an external trainer agreed to run a course for a youth agency, teaching youth workers how to lead discussion groups. The course was nonresidential and lasted three days. The mode of learning was primarily experiential. The trainer knew, therefore, that by the time the course ended at 5:00 P.M. each day, the participants would be very tired. The youth leaders worked mostly in clubs in the evening. The trainer realized this after the contract had been signed and sent a memo to the agency director pointing this out and asking for all participants to be released from evening duty for the duration of the course.

The first day of the course went very well. The second day went well, too, until midafternoon. Participants began to grumble at being made to work too hard and criticized the course design. During discussion it became clear that almost all of them were working that evening, as indeed they had done the previous evening. One had even asked her supervisor for the evening off and had been refused. Apparently the agency director had not followed through on the trainer's request.

The trainer was fortunate that the real reason for the hostility had emerged. If it had not, the course would have gone downhill from that point on, with the trainer wondering what was wrong with the course design. What can we learn from this?

The trainer made two basic mistakes. The first was not to follow through with the request to the agency director. The second mistake was not to clarify participant expectations regarding the course. This is part of developing the contract during the course and constitutes Stage 3.

Trainer's Tip: Get as much control as you can of communication to participants. Try to write course description information yourself.

Stage 3: Between trainers and participants

Because contact with participants up until this point has been through only the contractor, this stage is vital to the success of the course.

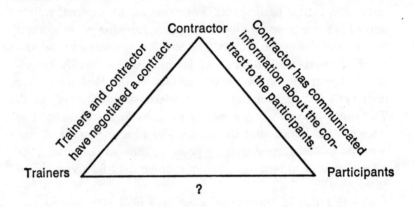

Just what do the participants think the contract is?

The question, of course, is just *what* has the contractor communicated to the participants? No matter how clear the negotiated contract is, and even if some control is kept on what is communicated to the participants, trainers should always check out the contract at the beginning of a course. We have come across examples of contracts that have even given the trainers control of all written information to participants, but then rumors or off-the-cuff remarks by the contractor have led to extraordinary fantasies on the part of the participants.

For example, an external training organization was to run a course on counseling skills for high school teachers. The contract with the high school principals seemed clear enough. The trainers wrote to the participants informing them of the course objectives and the mode of training. What the trainers did not know was that these teachers had previously been sent to a "communications" course, which, in fact, turned out to be a sensitivity training group. The teachers had not expected this, and, in addition, the course had been conducted in a very manipulative manner, with the participants being "set up" in a highly threatening way. The principals knew of this but had not informed the trainers. The teachers felt that they were now in for a similar experience. They simply did not believe the information sent to them by the trainers. Fortunately, the trainers checked out expectations on the first morning and clarified them, thus putting the participants at ease.

Trainer's Tip: A contract is a living thing. It is an initial reference point with the contractor and remains so until the end. But in between, the details have to be developed with the participants and constantly evaluated either formally or informally.

A CONTRACTING CHECKLIST

There follows a checklist that we have found useful to work through during the contracting process. Attending to these points eventually gets to be second nature, but the list is useful until that happens. You, as a trainer, will probably be able to add your own questions to it, as it must reflect your style and personality and the idiosyncrasies of the organizations you work with. The checklist is followed by a point-by-point discussion regarding its use.

CONTRACTING CHECKLIST

1. What does the contractor really want?
   a. Is it a training problem?
   b. Who is the actual client?
   c. Is he or she really a potential contractor?
   d. Can he or she specify the desired outcomes?

2. What information do you need?
    a. About the scope of the training
        How many participants will be involved?
        How much time will you have to do the training?
        What facilities are there?
        What resources are available?
        What budget do you have?
        What are the norms about training in the organization?
        Can it be serial or block training?
    b. About the participants
        What is the history of the training problem?
        Have they been involved before?
        Will they be volunteers or sent?
        Who chooses them?
    c. About the organization
        Who provides the budget?
        What company policies do you need to know?
        Are there any company politics you need to know?
        What is the management style?
    d. About control
        Who is responsible for communicating with the participants?
        Who decides on the contents of the training program?
        Is the decision on how it is to be run assigned? To whom?
        Who chooses the location?
        Who evaluates the training program?
3. What are your capabilities?
    a. Do you have the expertise?
    b. Do you have the necessary resources?
    c. Is staff available to you?
    d. Are your related experiences adequate?
4. What are your interests?
    a. Why might you accept the job?
        Money
        Professional development
        Personal development

   Future business
   Public relations exercise
   Social concern
   Enjoyment
  b. Why might you reject the job?
   A negative feeling about some or all of the above
   Conflict of interests and values
   Concern about your reputation
   Stress limits
   Unhappy over control (see 2 d)
   Concern about being "set up" or "used"
   Basically not a training problem

5. What is your decision?
 a. Yes
 b. No. (Always try to give alternatives. Never send a contractor away totally empty-handed.)

6. What is your proposal?
 a. Present some alternatives
 b. Select one alternative as a proposal. This should cover:
  Training outcomes (information, attitudes, behavior)
  Participants (number, types, selection procedures)
  Training procedures (time schedule, facilities, activities, serial or block)
  Staff (who, selection, training)
  Budget (how much, how it is to be divided, when payment takes place)
  Evaluation (how, is a report required, who evaluates)

7. Should you negotiate if the contractor proposes changes?
 a. Are changes within your capabilities (including time)?
 b. Can you make them within the budget?
 c. Is the contractor asking for major changes that require a new proposal?
 d. If so, is it worth it? (Don't be greedy. Do not accept at any cost just because you want the business or you don't wish to offend.)

8. How formal is your contract?
 a. As a minimum, have the major points written down.

(The degree of formality often depends on whether the contract is in-house or external, the scope of the training, budget size, the organization's policy, and your relationships with it.)

b. Include any changes resulting from your negotiation.

USING THE CONTRACTING CHECKLIST

We will now look at each item on the Contracting Checklist in turn and explore what is involved.

What does the contractor really want?

IS IT A TRAINING PROBLEM?

Example: We were approached by a small manufacturing firm to mount a course on communications skills for all the senior managers. We found it difficult to discover what the managing director really wanted except that he thought it would be "good" for all his managers. This kind of general objective is often the presenting problem, as it disguises the underlying issue. This sometimes happens because the contractor is not yet sure about being totally open with you, because he or she is trying to fool someone else, or—the most usual reason—because the contractor has not worked it through.

After further exploration it became clear to us that the real problem in this situation was one senior manager, who was a brilliant engineer but antagonized most people who worked under him. The question then became one of deciding whether the best solution would be to run an expensive training course for all senior managers in the hope that this one manager would get feedback, acquire new skills, and mend his ways or to treat it more like an organizational problem and work just with this manager and his team. The latter course, which was less expensive and more direct, was subsequently chosen.

Trainer's Tip: Can you find any other way of solving this problem? Does it really demand a training solution?

WHO IS THE ACTUAL CLIENT?

A training organization was contacted by the personnel supervisor of a large department store to provide some training courses for the store's retail staff on how to deal with difficult customers. The contracting had got as far as formulating a proposal when the personnel supervisor phoned the trainers and said that the store manager wished to meet them. At the meeting the store manager amazed them by telling them that their proposed training course would not work in this store, and, anyway, he had better things to spend his money on. The personnel supervisor had been using the trainers to make a point to the store manager, thinking they might convince him better of the need for training than she could. Unfortunately, the trainers had spent weeks putting the proposal together—all wasted work because they had not discovered who the real contractor was.

Trainer's Tip: Does your contractor have the power to contract? If not, find out who does.

IS HE OR SHE REALLY A POTENTIAL CONTRACTOR?

It is possible to spend hours on the telephone or with people whose only motives are to get ideas from you so that they can either do it themselves or get someone else to do it. Unless this is part of your job, can you afford to spend this amount of time or give away expertise? If you choose to do so because it is a worthy cause, that is one thing. We are talking about the situation in which you are strung along unknowingly. This is a difficult dilemma to get into. It may be a contractor who simply takes time to make up his or her mind. In such a case the solution is to say that you have established fees for consulting time, however low the rates may be. Another solution is to ask for a request or proposal on paper. If the contractor is not serious, you probably will not hear from him or her again.

CAN HE OR SHE SPECIFY THE DESIRED OUTCOMES?

Contractors typically talk in terms of problems, which is understandable. It is much more difficult to get them to talk in terms of outcomes, or objectives. But this is essential. Once you have agreed with them on the outcomes, you can go ahead. The objectives need to be as specific as possible. They will usually involve conveying information, changing attitudes, or changing behavior.

Nonspecific Outcomes	Specific Outcomes
Better selling techniques	An increase in the ability to contact new customers (up to 20 percent), make sales (20 percent), and get reorders.
Gain computer knowledge	To be able to define the different types of computer systems available, describe their advantages and disadvantages, and pinpoint the ways in which a specific computer system could help this organization.
Improve communication techniques	To identify and remove existing barriers to communication in the organization, and to help managers improve their skills in building relationships and in sending and receiving messages.

What information do you need?

ABOUT THE SCOPE OF THE TRAINING

Information on the scope of the training is vital. It is all too easy to talk grandiosely about outcomes and then realize with horror that the contractor has four hundred people to go through your design that accommodates thirty.

You know that it is vital for the participants to attend all sessions. You know the design; the contractor doesn't. The importance will have to be spelled out.

Trainer's Tip: Don't expect a contractor to be familiar with training techniques in general and your training techniques in particular.

In the desire to get a new client, it is sometimes tempting to reduce the budget before making program changes, especially if the budget initially frightens the client. Sometimes this may be appropriate, but rarely before setting up a program do you know how much money you need to run it. You don't earn extra respect for being cheap. On the contrary, often you earn more respect by asking a higher price—not that we are recommending that as a general practice. If you cut your budget, you may start to feel resentful, you may not be able to get the staff or facilities you want, the course is less likely to be successful, and so your client will not be satisfied anyway!

Trainer's Tip: Don't undercut your budget.

ABOUT THE PARTICIPANTS

Find out what kinds of training the potential participants have undergone previously. If they have had any bad or boring experiences, this is likely to have created a negative "training set." Your design will have to take into account overcoming this quickly when the course starts. This was discussed under checking out expectations (page 31).

You need to know what training modes they are used to. If they have experienced only a lecture format, you might think twice before starting off the course with a sensitivity exercise that enables them to introduce themselves to one another nonverbally! We are not saying that you should never take risks, but we are saying that you should know what risks you are taking.

It is vital to discover whether participants are used to being reported on individually to management after the course. It is also essential for you to clear this issue with the organization. If you agree not to report back, stick to your agreement.

We have always found it essential to know how the participants are to be selected. The all-important factor of motivation is something you must have data on before designing your course. You can run successful courses when attendance is required, and you will have a better chance of success if you can build procedures into your design that take account of this.

You need to know how long you can have the participants. It is at this stage where your jaw drops as you realize that all those major attitudinal and behavioral changes have to take place in a half day or two half days!

ABOUT THE ORGANIZATION

Find out who is providing the budget. That person is ultimately your contractor. Make sure that the contractor knows and approves what you are doing.

Does the content of the training dovetail with general company policy? If you are an external trainer, you are often at the mercy of the internal training or personnel department and will be seeing the organization through their eyes. Try to ensure that you get an opportunity to talk with other senior people in the organization to get a wider perspective.

Trainer's Tip: Find out if you are being used to fight someone else's battles.

This is just as important for in-house training.

Find out about the major styles of management in operation. Are the people used to a very task-oriented style or to a person-oriented style, to being told, sold, delegated to, or engaged in mutual problem solving? This will be important to your design.

Trainer's Tip: Always ensure that you get more than one perspective on the organization.

ABOUT CONTROL FACTORS

You must have full agreement early on as to who decides which participants will attend the course, who they are to be, their past experience and training, and the mix of status and expertise.

One unpopular senior manager among a group of junior managers could ruin the learning climate.

Try to get some control of the communication to the participants. Write the course handout and publicity, if possible, or at least a first draft for the contractor to rewrite, but get an agreement to have it checked out with you before circulation.

At this stage, too, you need to clarify how much control you have over the content of the course and how it will be run. If you have any special demands for facilities and resources, express them at this point.

How will the contractor evaluate the course? Ensure that you are brought into discussions aimed at determining the criteria for success. These, in turn, should feed back into your design. Defining criteria for success is an additional procedure for clarifying desired outcomes. As such you need to be part of it.

Trainer's Tip: Find out as much as you can about the participants.

What are your capabilities?

This is a difficult question to answer honestly. We find that many trainers think they are capable of doing anything. Be realistic. Don't take on a project if you have not first checked out that you can get the appropriate staff, that you have the necessary materials and equipment, and that it relates to an area of past experience. For example, a free-lance consultant was delighted to land a contract with a large distillery company. The job included teaching consulting skills to the entire management structure— about 350. She took the contract and only then proceeded to try to sign up additional free-lance staff to help her run the programs. She couldn't get the staff and ended up running ten identical residential training programs of five days' duration in five months. This almost wrecked her marriage and did cause her to break down under the stress.

Obviously, for your own development and excitement, you will sometimes want to take on jobs that are very new or different. But ensure that you have access to good resources and that you have enough planning time to build a totally new course.

Trainer's Tip: Learning to say no is your most important survival skill.

What are your interests?

Don't be greedy! Don't be seduced by simply being asked.

We recently recorded the decision-making process when someone called asking for assistance to run a consulting skills course for a group of personnel managers. Having worked through the previous three areas on the checklist satisfactorily, we came to the point of personal interest.

"How badly do we want to do it?" "Very much." "Why do we want to do it?" "They pay our top rates; we've worked with them before, and it will be enjoyable to make contact with some of the people again. In addition, it will help keep our names current in the organization. It will almost certainly lead to further consulting skills courses, and maybe even on to new horizons. We also believe that industry will be a better place to work in if these skills are more widely distributed.

"In terms of the checklist (page 60), the factors of money, professional development, personal development, future business, public relations, social concern, and enjoyment all feature. In terms of item 4 b, we also know that it *is* a training issue, that we will be able to control communication to participants and the design and mode of learning of the training, that we will have some say in location, and that we will be involved in evaluation. We will not have control over who comes, but we trust our contractor has prior experience of the type of course we run. We are busy at the moment, but because this is a fairly standard course, it will involve a minimum of preparatory work and ongoing stress while in progress.

"Consequently, our answer is yes."

Trainer's Tip: Always ask yourself, what's in this for me? What are the personal costs of failure?

What is your decision?

We recommend that you never send someone away completely empty-handed. If you cannot, or do not wish to, take the job, try to think of other people who might fit the bill. We like to do this for both social and selfish reasons. Social, because we believe it's desirable to help people wherever possible. Selfish, because the contractors will have a good image of us and because the people whom we recommended might someday reciprocate.

What is your proposal?

It is often advisable to present more than one proposal. This demonstrates flexibility and ability and is especially useful if there are budgeting problems. However, don't spend too much time producing too great a range of alternatives, since this can be confusing.

If an organization really wants the program, it will rarely turn it down on budget grounds. However, it might well come back to you with a plea to cut it, so have some ideas in mind. For example, cut out the residential factor, ask the participants to pay for their own meals, and ask their secretaries to prepare your materials (this enables you to reduce your fees, and although you are still costing the employee time, it is not new money). You could also consider cutting down on your preparation fee, and so on. However, your budget should include these expenditures:

Trainer's conducting fees (hourly or daily basis)
Trainer's preparation fees (hourly or daily basis)
Trainer's expenses—travel, accommodations
Adjunct staff fees and expenses—technicians, clerical help
Cost of materials—film, and so on
Overhead charges

The relative importance of these expenditures will depend on whether you are an in-house or external trainer.

A particularly difficult item for many trainers in presenting a proposal is naming a conducting and preparation fee. Always ask for what you think you should get. If you anticipate that the organization cannot afford it, you are never giving yourself the chance to find out if you do not ask. If you work in a new area or for a new organization, you sometimes have no idea what the going rate is. Ask colleagues for the going rate, or try to get an idea from people with more experience. Confer with a contact person in the organization as to what the usual fee would be. We don't recommend this except as a final resort. It gives the impression that you are inexperienced and are uncertain as to how much you are worth. Remember to ask for preparation fees—but also remember that it is not the organization's responsibility to underwrite your professional development. It might take you five days, but perhaps you should charge for only one or two days. After all, you are building up your repertoire for the future.

Your budget proposal should also be clear as to when and how payment will take place. Who is responsible for paying other trainers and adjunct staff?

As an in-house trainer it is often valuable to budget for your own time. This can be useful data to have when pushing for a senior management decision on your training operation. It also helps you evaluate the use of your own time on a cost-effectiveness basis.

Should you negotiate if the contractor proposes changes?

If the contractor objects to your proposal or tries to make changes, you will have to decide whether or not to negotiate. Much depends upon how much you want the contract.

This can be a valuable moment in contracting. As a result of the contractor's response, you realize, for example, that what you thought the contractor wanted is not what was wanted at all. The frustrating part is that sometimes the contractor needs to see a firm proposal before knowing what he or she really wants.

How formal is your contract?

Get it in writing! The reasons for this were spelled out earlier.

To prevent such conflicts as "But I thought we'd agreed that you would provide the materials and I'd provide the equipment!" it is essential at this stage to include any changes resulting from your negotiations after presenting proposals.

One of the major reasons for courses not working is that the contract was not right in the first place between trainer and contractor, contractor and participants, and trainer and participants. We are still surprised at how often mistakes that we make or that we hear of are traceable to the initial contract.

Trainer's Tip: Remember, a proposal is not a contract.

---

5 Designing the Course

AN ILLUSTRATED CASE

With the contract signed and sealed, we come to the nitty-gritty of designing the course. This means designing and sequencing learning events, choosing and developing teaching procedures and materials, and planning for the best learning climate. But prior to this comes the operational clarification of desired outcomes, which helps us define our purposes and keeps us on target.

Rather than designing a variety of courses throughout this chapter, we have chosen to use only one example and to follow that course through in depth. We start at the moment of contact and follow it through the design phase.

A medium-sized engineering firm contacted us and asked for a course in communications skills for its senior management. The suggestion was that the managing director (who made the initial contract), the entire board of directors, and all the senior management personnel should attend. This amounted to twenty-eight people. We were impressed by the managing director, visited the firm and liked the "feel" of the place, met some of the directors, and were impressed by their eagerness to join in the course like everyone else. We agreed with the managing director on a four-day course—a block of three days and an additional follow-up day three weeks later. We obtained background information on the participants individually. We agreed on an approximate budget, which allowed us to hire another trainer, and on the type of facilities required and that the contractor should find these and then we would check them out. We discovered that most of the participants had not been involved in anything remotely like this before and that there would likely be some apprehension and fantasies. We agreed to produce an outline of this course, its objectives, and the methods. This was to be used by the managing director as the basis of a course description. He would check this out with us before sending it to the participants.

Evaluation was to be ongoing—at the end of the three-day course and by questionnaire one month after the fourth day. In addition, the managing director would assess any improvement in the performance of the three managers who were particularly poor at communications, and all participants would assess any improvement in working climate generally, and communications in particular.

We had control over content but agreed to check the design out in advance with the managing director, whom we could use as a resource to alert us to special problems and conditions. We also insisted on a veto over location and agreed that it should be away from the firm's premises.

We wanted to accept the invitation, as the money was good and it would be a challenge to put together a new program, devising new training techniques that would be then available for future use. In addition, we were attracted to working with an entire management team in contrast with our most common type of course, which consisted of strangers from a variety of firms.

We had run many courses related to communications skills and felt that it would not be too time consuming to adapt previous material for use in this course and to create new techniques that would feed back into other courses. We had access to a colleague with whom we had worked on a number of occasions. We all enjoyed working together, and there was total mutual trust. To run the course, we would almost certainly require videotaping equipment; and from previous courses, we knew of a good resource for this—a firm familiar with our style of working from which we could hire the equipment quite inexpensively.

You will recall from chapter 4 that we have been working our way through the Contracting Checklist (page 59). We have reached the point of presenting a proposal, which we did and immediately ran into budget problems. We budgeted for fees for two days' preparation time and for three trainers plus residential expenses for four training days. We knew that the preparation would take longer than two days, but we felt that that was our problem and not the organization's. We needed to put together a whole new course, and they should not be paying for our learning. The managing director, who was unfamiliar with training programs, by now had some figures on how much it would cost him to put twenty-eight people in a hotel for three nights. The final figure horrified him. In addition, he had received negative feedback from some of the managers who were worried about (1) being away from their families for three to four nights and (2) leaving the firm without any of the management team for four days. Because we were eager to do the work, we were prepared to negotiate. We waived our two days' preparation fee (extremely unusual and not to be recommended) and agreed to run the course from 9:00 A.M. to 9:00 P.M. locally so that participants could return home each night. In addition, we timed the three-day course for Thursday, Friday, and Saturday, thereby taking up only two working days. We also said that we would consider designing the course so that half of the participants would go to work on Friday morning and the other half would return to work on Friday afternoon, with the entire group meeting again on Friday evening. An in-training day was planned for three weeks later as a review/follow-up day. The agreement was finally put on paper and signed.

Our contract was now complete, and we were free to begin designing the program itself.

MAKING GOALS SPECIFIC

Take the general outcomes agreed to in the contract and brainstorm for each of these in as many specific ways as you can to demonstrate that the goal has been achieved.

We find it useful to distinguish between three kinds of outcomes: learning facts and concepts (information), learning skills and competencies (behavior), and developing values and beliefs (attitudes).

To help in this process we suggest using the Goal Analysis Work Sheet. This has been filled in with an example from the communication skills course. Courses typically have rather vague goals, such as improving communications at all levels in the organization. We have included only two of the several goals.

The goals represent *your* purpose or objectives. The outcomes are more specific and provide indications of what must happen for goals to be achieved. When describing goals and outcomes, always think in terms of the participants, not the trainers. For example, the first goal listed is to learn conflict-resolution procedures. *Teaching* is the procedure you will use to help participants learn. The goal is for them to learn, not for you to teach. Ultimately your concern is that they learn and implement the conflict-resolution procedure, regardless of how they do it. They might read a book or see a film. Because trainers are necessarily engulfed by the teaching function, it is easy to forget that the real goal of instruction is learning, not teaching. So always review your goal statements to ensure that they focus on the learner.

Trainer's Tip: Goals and outcomes refer to learners, not teachers.

Outcome statements should refer to things, people, or behaviors that you can observe or at least infer. In other words, they should be operational. Obviously you can't see or touch an attitude, but you can infer its existence from observing behavior. In the example on the work sheet, each information and behavior outcome refers to something that exists. In that sense it is specific and has the same meaning for all concerned.

Trainer's Tip: The first stage in design is to translate goals into specific outcomes of information, behavior, or attitudes.

GOAL ANALYSIS WORK SHEET

GOAL	
	INFORMATION
1. Learn and implement conflict-resolution procedure.	Principles of conflict resolution.
2. Increase amount and quality of feedback between managers.	Understand principles of feedback. Understand criteria regarding when to provide feedback. Understand criteria regarding when to request feedback.

NOTE: Both goals refer to specific content; that is, the instruction is concerned with a particular method for resolving conflicts, and the feedback tools, such as probing and confronting, are described in written materials. Thus these outcomes have real-world referents and are not just vague terms.

OUTCOMES	
BEHAVIOR	ATTITUDES
Ability to describe conflict-resolution procedure.	Conflicts are useful indicators of problems.
	Conflict has causes.
Use conflict-resolution behavior in three simulations.	Conflicts can be resolved.
	Compromise is an effective tool.
Use conflict-resolution behavior on the job.	
Describe without accusing.	Positive criticism is helpful.
Convey with clarity.	Others' views can be useful.
Check perception.	
Probe without offending.	Free to evaluate feed-back from others.
Confront congenially.	Don't need to defend actions.
	Expressing positive thoughts and feelings is useful.

THE CONTEXT PROFILE

The first stage of design has dealt with specifying the outcomes of the program. The next stage is the consideration of all the environmental factors that surround the program and that must be known before designing it. We refer to this as the *context* of the program and have found the following factors important. As you design your program, the description and implications column will help you.

CONTEXT PROFILE

FACTOR	DESCRIPTION
In-house/external trainer	
Budget	
Time available	
Block or serial	
Participants' training history	
Voluntary or forced	
One-shot or ongoing	
Homogeneous or heterogeneous	
Open or closed	
Facilities	
Staff	
On site or off site	
Residential or nonresidential	

It would be useful to examine each context condition.

In-house or external trainer

An in-house trainer and an external trainer each have advantages and disadvantages. What effect on your program would an external trainer have compared with someone who is part of the organization? The advantages of being an in-house trainer:

• You know the system and are familiar with the politics.

IMPLICATIONS Positive and Negative

- You speak the language of the organization (though there can sometimes be some big differences among departments within a large organization).

- You understand the norms.

- You identify with the organization's needs and goals. If the organization benefits from a course, so will you.

- You are known. You do not represent the threat of an unfamiliar outside force.

- You know the site, who does what, who needs to be "chatted up" to get the course running smoothly.

The disadvantages of being an in-house trainer:

- You may lack an objective perspective.
- You may not have the special knowledge or skill required.
- You may not have the credibility. Prophets in their own land sometimes are dead losses!
- You may be hindered by past history. You may have to live down past failures or even hostility generated by past successes.
- You may not have the time.
- Participants may find it difficult to see you as a trainer when they are used to you as a colleague.

Sometimes, even though you have the skills and resources, there may be advantages to bringing in an external trainer.

Budget

Have you taken into account all possible budget details: staff fees, staff expenses, cost of materials, fees for additional consultants, participants' expenses, equipment hire, and non-out-of-pocket costs, such as participants' time? Have you considered ways of cutting down on your budget?

Time available

How much time do you have? Can you negotiate further time, such as for a follow-up if necessary?

Block or serial

Do you need the participants together for a single block of time, or would you prefer several shorter sessions? Before beginning your design, be clear on how flexible you can be. This, of course, may have been determined at the contract phase. Advantages of block design:

- Buildup of motivation and involvement.
- Minimum interference from back-home factors.
- Easier to build good learning climate.
- Just one block of time in the trainer's program.
- Minimum warm-up problems.

Advantages of serial design:

- Homework assignments can be used.
- Opportunity for participants to relate the learning back to the organization and report on this at subsequent training sessions.
- Opportunity for trainers to check back with the organization to see if the course is on the right lines.

Participants' training history

If the participants have had some good training experiences, you will be commencing the course with people ready to learn. Bad prior experiences can lead to suspicion and hostility.

Voluntary or forced

Volunteers usually make for less exhausting courses! However, some of the most successful courses we have run have begun with hostility, but when that was openly dealt with, participants have become totally committed.

When participants have to be there, it is most important to check out their expectations early. Negative feelings can usually be suppressed for a limited period of time. They are fuel for sabotage.

One-shot or ongoing

Is the training course a one-time event, or will it be repeated? Often it's difficult to know. The contractor may intend for it to be one-shot, but a successful course could lead to your being asked to repeat it or do other courses.

Homogeneous or heterogeneous

The composition of the group should be in line with the objectives. If you want a wide range of ideas and experience, you require a heterogeneous group. If you want a common understanding and similar motivaton, you will be better off with a homogeneous group. On the whole, homogeneous groups are probably easier to design for and manage.

Open or closed

Can participants join or leave the course at different stages? Can they come and go? If they can, you have an open group. Advantages of an open group:

- Can accommodate people with different time schedules.

- Continuous flow of new ideas and energy.

- Less intense than a closed group.

Disadvantages of an open group:

- Participants are at different stages psychologically.

- Repetition is often necessary, and this can be boring for some.

- Managing materials is more difficult.

Trainer's Tip: A voluntary, homogeneous, closed group is usually the easiest to design for and manage. However, what is easiest is not always the most effective.

Facilities

What physical facilities are available?

- Room large enough for general sessions?
- Sufficient number of small rooms?
- Bright and cheery rooms?
- Arrangements for eating and breaks?

- Appropriate teaching equipment?
- Adequate heating and ventilation?
- Comfortable seating?
- Freedom from distractions and interruptions?

The nature of the building itself is important. Does it convey the message you want to convey? If not, can you counter the message in any way?

We like running courses in open, rural settings or overlooking the ocean or a river, with a swimming pool; tennis, squash, and racquet ball courts; a sauna and gymnasium! But it is possible to overcome the grimmest or strangest surroundings. The oddest course that one of us has run was in a convent in Newcastle in the industrial northeast of England. We had flip charts strategically covering pictures of the stations of the cross, a tape recorder playing music from the altar, and meals prepared by an order of nuns devoted to total silence. In fact, we were able to use the surroundings to our advantage by enjoying the incongruity of it all—being unconventional in a convent. However, running a course is difficult enough without making things harder for yourself with facilities that work against you.

Staff

How many staff members are available to you and who are they? Do they need any training or orientation? Are any being forced on you? Are personality clashes likely?

On site or off site

Advantages of an off-site course:

- Away from normal everyday distractions—one's work environment can constantly remind one of work.
- Can reduce the possibility of interruptions from phone calls and job problems.
- Demonstrates real commitment from the organization.

Disadvantages of an off-site course:

- Participants could object to traveling or, if residential, being away from home.
- Cannot keep in touch with ongoing work.

Residential or nonresidential

Residential courses are usually more conducive to a better climate, but they are sometimes unpopular with participants who don't want to be away from home.

What follows is an example of a completed Context Profile for the communications course whose history we are following.

COMPLETED CONTEXT PROFILE

FACTOR	DESCRIPTION
In-house or external trainer	External.
Budget	Four training days, three trainers. No preparation fee. Fee for hiring a technician and videotape recorder.
Time available	Four days, from 9:00 A.M. to 9:00 P.M. Nonresidential.
Block or serial	Three days block and one day three weeks later.
Participants' training history	Must not have been on any behavioral course before.
Voluntary or forced	Participants will be invited, though they will not really be able to refuse.
One-shot or ongoing	One-shot.
Homogeneous or heterogeneous	Homogeneous.

	IMPLICATIONS Positive and Negative
	Trainers could deal with some interpersonal relationship problems that internal people would find difficult.
	Prepared to accept no preparation fee, as we really want the job.
	Prompt morning starts may be difficult.
	The gap will enable a review, follow-up, and homework possibilities.
	Nothing way out. Use basic self-awareness procedures.
	Danger of people feeling that this is being thrust on them.
	There will be only four days to achieve the desired outcomes.
	They all work for the same firm and are senior managers.

COMPLETED CONTEXT PROFILE (continued)	
FACTOR	DESCRIPTION
Open or closed	Closed.
Facilities	Motel.
Staff	Three trainers, one technician.
On site or off site	Off site.
Residential or nonresidential	Nonresidential.

PROCEDURES, STRUCTURES, AND MATERIALS

We are now clear on our training goals, and we know all we need to know about the context in which the training will take place. The next series of decisions revolve around the following points:

Teaching procedures to be used
Teaching structures to be used
Teaching materials to be used
Important factors to be considered before choosing a procedure or structure

Teaching procedures

The main teaching procedures available to you are summarized in the Teaching Procedures Checklist on page 88. There are numerous variations on these. You may also use different titles for some of the procedures.

Each procedure is rated according to three criteria:

The length of time it takes to develop or organize it in advance.
The cost.
Are participants involved actively, or do they sit passively and receive?

	IMPLICATIONS
	Good control.
	Good food and training conditions. Flexible coffee breaks.
	Exactly what the staff requires. All four have worked together previously.
	This will be essential for senior management who otherwise may be called away.
	There may be a danger of breaking the flow of the course, but at least it should run late enough each night to minimize back-home interactions!

We have filled in these checklist columns, but only as a general guide. For example, a lecture is high in development time only initially, and there is possible subsequent use. It should be understood that these represent our experience and judgments. Others may differ.

Some of these procedures are clear to all of us, but others may need the brief explanation that follows.

PRESENTATION

Lecture The lecture form of presentation is the oldest of all teaching procedures. It does take time to develop, but the time is reasonable. It is important to remember that a thirty-minute lecture is probably all that people can take without having it interspersed with something else.

By making the lecture two-way—inviting the participants to ask questions at any time—you can increase the activity dimension. The participants will become more involved if there is good use of overhead transparencies, filmstrips, tapes, and the like. Skilled lecturers often warm up their audience with a joke or anecdote and consciously use humor to maintain interest.

It is vital to have your lecture prepared in advance, with key issues pinpointed. Have these on a flip chart or overhead projector,

TEACHING PROCEDURES CHECKLIST

PROCEDURE	TIME TO DEVELOP	MATERIAL COST	PASSIVE OR ACTIVE
1. *Presentation*			
Lecture	High	Low	P
Lecturette	High	Low	P
Microteaching	High	Low	P/A
Debate	Med	Low	P/A
2. *Demonstration*			
Showing	High	Low	P
Coaching	Low	Low	A/P
Rehearsing	Low	Low	A/P
3. *Group Learning*			
Skills practice	High	Low	A
Discussion	Low	Low	A
Structured discussion	Med	Low	A
Panel	Med	Low	A/P
Seminar	Med	Low	A
Brainstorming	Low	Low	A
Buzz groups	Low	Low	A
Problem-solving group	Med	Low	A
Learning/teaching team	Med	Low	A
4. *Individual Learning*			
Reading	High	Low	P
Preparation	Low/High	Low	P
5. *Structured Experiences*			
Role playing	High	High/Med	A/P
Drama	High	Low	A/P
Case study	High	Med	A
Critical incident	High	Low	A
In-basket	High	Med	A/P
Exercises	High	Low/Med	A
Games	High	Med/High	A

or use a handout. This demonstrates care and concern for the learner as well as competence in the subject.

Preferably do not read your notes. Have headings on a series of cards or a sheet.

Lecturette This is a minilecture, approximately ten to fifteen minutes in length. It is often given after a skills practice or experiential session in order to make some teaching points.

Microteaching After a teaching point is made, the group is asked to discuss it in small groups in an unstructured or structured way. The participants report back their discussion, the trainer deals with any points raised and then continues with his or her next point, the group splits again, and so on.

You get through less material when you use this method, but you can be more sure that it is understood.

Debate This method can be fun or frustrating and usually is both. Sometimes real learning can be prevented by a determination to destroy the other person's argument. However, it can be a good climate builder, especially if the debate is conducted lightly by the participants. It makes a good evening activity after a heavy day.

DEMONSTRATION

Showing For really detailed work, you demonstrate slowly, step by step, how to do something, with the group watching you or a television screen.

Coaching You give the participants some instructions, stand by their sides while they do it, and give them some tips while they are doing it. Sometimes you don't even need to be at their sides. You can communicate via an ear transmitter that only you and the individual participant can hear. You can also use a time-out procedure: The participant learns the task, consults with the trainer or fellow participants, then returns to perform the task.

Rehearsing The participant spends time practicing what he or she is going to do and may even get feedback on the performance before trying it for real.

GROUP LEARNING

Skills practice The participant practices skills in front of fellow participants, usually receiving feedback on the performance. There will often be an opportunity for practicing again.

Discussion This is the most common form of group learning technique and also the most abused. Without any clear guidelines, the participants are often left to discuss something they have just heard about. Unless you are working with an experienced group, skilled in discussion techniques, we usually recommend making up a list of stimulus questions along with some guidelines of how to operate.

Structured discussion In addition to the above, you might suggest that each person have two minutes of uninterrupted time to voice his or her views, this to be followed with general discussion. You can ask people to write down some points first and then discuss them, possibly again using an equal-time technique. We have found that this helps build a good learning climate by emphasizing that each person's contribution is of value. You can ask each group to report back to a general session, and you might want to suggest that each group nominate a recorder, presenter, facilitator, chairperson, or any other role model you feel would contribute to the task.

Panel This technique is highly active for a few but passive for the majority. You can use a "touch panel" technique. At any stage, a member of the audience is allowed to touch the shoulder of a particular panel person, who then has to leave the panel and be replaced by the newcomer.

A panel usually works best if the participants have had time to prepare. You can ensure that different viewpoints are represented. Panel members can be guest experts who have particular knowledge or experiences, or they can be selected from your group.

Seminar The trainer leads a group discussion. A seminar usually assumes that the participants have a particular expertise, experience, or potential contribution to bring to the group. The success of this depends on the trainer's small-group leadership techniques, especially the ability to keep from lecturing and to get participants to take part. This is often improved by an ongoing group record of the discussion on flip charts, kept up by a recorder who is not the group leader.

Brainstorming The participants produce as many ideas as they can in a short period of time. Volume is what is desired. They should say anything that occurs to them, however silly it might sound. A recorder writes down every comment, including the funny ones. (These can often be quite revealing or good for climate building after the brainstorming.) The one important rule is that participants not discuss or evaluate. This is the best device we know for quickly finding out what a group knows or is thinking.

Buzz groups This usually consists of small discussion groups of four to six persons meeting for five to ten minutes with no leader. Often brief reports are brought back to a general session. It is a good way of getting instant participation, breaking up a lecture, or checking to see where a group is at.

Problem-solving group The groups are assigned a specific problem to diagnose or solve. This will be relevant to the learning objectives and may well involve feedback on their performance from the trainer or other groups.

Learning/teaching team One of the best ways of learning anything is by having to teach it to someone else. One group may have to pass on a skill to another group, or design an exercise, demonstration, or program to teach another course. It is highly involving and entertaining and can encourage friendly intergroup rivalry.

INDIVIDUAL LEARNING

Reading This can be precourse, during the course, or follow-up. Precourse reading, if available, is often a good idea as long as you do not assume that everyone will have done the reading. The only way of maximizing that possibility is by setting a precourse task that has to be brought, completed, to the first session. You can build reading time into a course, even if this only involves reading handouts. Trainers sometimes hand out reams of paper and expect the participants to read them in their spare time, which in some courses would mean after midnight! A serial design offers good opportunities for reading work to be done. It is recommended that you do not simply hand out a massive list of book titles to demonstrate how well read you are. Give a handout of the key titles with some explanation why these are essential reading.

Preparation Again, a serial design lends itself best to this. All forms of preparation, such as writing, data collecting, and practicing skills, outside the course are a crafty way of sneaking in extra participant time. Sometimes it is appropriate to program preparation time into a course. Get participant commitment to a contract before designing a session that relies on preparation work's having been done.

Preparation usually involves private work and some reporting back.

STRUCTURED EXPERIENCES

Role playing People practice skills, and explore ideas and feelings, in a situation that simulates a real-life experience. Participants can either choose or be assigned roles. Roles may be written or ad-libbed. The more prepared and structured the role play, the longer to introduce and to get going and the greater the likelihood of breakdown because someone has forgotten a vital piece of information.

You can role play entire situations or just a part of a situation. Using *role reversal,* you can get participants to play the role that is opposite the one they would normally play. *Multirole playing* involves the same participant's taking more than one role—perhaps switching roles, such as from customer to salesperson. *Mirroring* is a technique in which while some participants are role playing, other participants can move in and translate what a player has said into what he really meant to say. It is like being someone's alter ego.

Careful preparation is essential for success.

Drama Dramas involve more structure than role playing, and more time is needed for a group of volunteers to devise a drama to highlight a teaching point. The points made about role playing usually apply to dramas. One variation to encourage greater participation is to allow an observer to join either by tapping an existing actor on the shoulder and taking his or her place or by making an introduction as a new character in the drama.

Case study This is a detailed description of a situation or problem related to the learning objectives. This can be real or contrived and involves a group discussion of the case, with a trainer leading the discussion. The trainer can pass over group leadership. A fishbowl technique can also be used (page 94) whereby one group discusses a case and then another group evaluates the discussion or even takes over and continues it while in turn being observed.

A variation is the minicase study, which presents a brief situation for the group to resolve. It could be a study of a problem such as "Your secretary has turned up late for the third time this week; what are you going to do?"

Critical incident This illustrates only the most important or most dramatic issue of a case.

"The customer has begun yelling at the top of his voice that he demands to see the manager. The manager, when requested by the salesperson to see the customer, says she is too busy. What can the salesperson do?"

A discussion is then led by the trainer on the various options open to the salesperson. The trainer should have some definite alternatives ready to share at a later stage if not anticipated by the discussion. This procedure is usually more concerned with the skill of getting at the roots of a problem than with the knowledge needed to solve it.

Large groups can be divided, and each smaller group can report back on its conclusions.

In-basket This is a type of case study in which letters, memos, telephone messages, company statements, and so forth, are given to a participant and he or she is asked to perform the role of manager, union leader, or the like. The participant has to write actual responses to the items in the in-basket. The same set of items can be given to all participants, who can carry out the exercise simultaneously. At the end the participants can form groups to discuss their work. A staff member can supervise each group discussion if appropriate. In-basket procedures are often relatively complex in design.

Exercises Exercises usually involve participants' generating data about themselves or solving a case study or simulated problem. One of their main strengths is that they encourage active involvement of all participants in the learning experience. Typically, an exercise will have a clearly defined objective and a set time limit, and it will involve participants in individual or group work, which is then discussed or evaluated by themselves or with the trainer. Any exercise, in our opinion, should always conclude with a general session at which teaching points are summarized and participants' reactions monitored. We believe that a trainer should not run an exercise unless he or she has participated in it before or in an exercise very similar to it.

Trainer's Tip: Most people can start a group off on an exercise. The skill comes in knowing how to draw the learning from the experience together for the participants.

Games   There are an increasing number of games manufactured for training purposes. But in addition to games involving such things as boards and cards, games can be created by trainers to make teaching points in a fun atmosphere. Tutor-group or individual competition can be utilized to ensure that people learn. Two reasons for using games are to achieve a learning objective and to build the right learning climate.

Teaching structures

When you have decided on your teaching procedures, there often remains an additional decision about how you are going to physically organize the participants and the staff during the teaching. Some procedures, such as in-basket, automatically dictate structures. Others allow flexibility. Here is a list of structures used, with explanations.

TEACHING STRUCTURES CHECKLIST

Participant Structures

Total group	The entire course is brought together in one group.
Small groups	The course is split into groups of four to ten.
Pairs	Each person is asked to choose a partner. In odd-numbered groups, a staff member can pair up or one trio can be used.
Trios	If your course numbers do not divide evenly by three, one or more quartets or pairs can be used.
Fishbowl	One group performs while another watches. Typically, the groups would then change around.
Circle	Entire group, including the staff, sits in a circle.
Horseshoe	Entire group sits in a semicircle open at one end, where the staff members sit or stand.
Rows	Rows are for sardines or large public lectures, not for training courses!
Table group	Entire group meets around a table.
Intergroup	Groups are engaged in competitive activities.

Simultaneous activities	While one group is doing one thing, another group is doing something else—not unlike a three-ring circus.
Options	Groups may choose from a series of options available to them. Sometimes this can result in simultaneous activities.
Change around	Participants change groups. This enables them to meet more people.

Staff Structures

Single leader	Only one staff member working, even though there may be others on the staff.
Joint leaders	More than two staff members working together.
Up front	Staff member is the focus of the group, either sitting conspicuously or standing.
Facilitating group	Acts as a discussion leader, not making any inputs.
Consultant	Is available to groups or wanders from group to group.
Coordinator	Coordinates simultaneous activities or different group discussions.
Participant	Staff member is not up front and participates in the learning activity.

Teaching materials

On the next page we list a variety of teaching materials assessed in terms of time taken to develop, cost, and whether their use calls for participants to be active or passive.

Here follows a list of our suggestions for using different materials:

- Don't use materials to show off. Everything used must be justifiable in terms of the learning objectives and climate building.

- Try to minimize your requirements for technological expertise. Videotape recorders break down, film projectors require yards of cable that people trip over, slide projectors require

MATERIALS	TIME TO DEVELOP	MATERIAL COST	ACTIVE OR PASSIVE
Films	High	High	P
Videotapes	High	High	P
Overhead transparencies	High	Med	P
Slides	High	High	P
Tapes	High	Med	P
Tests	Med	High	A
Questionnaires	High/Med	Med	A
Handouts	High	Low	P
Posters, flip charts, chalkboards, masking tape	Med/Low	Low	P
Name tags	Low	Low	P
Notebooks	Low	Low	A/P

slides to be arranged, tape recorders need mikes good enough to pick up voices, transparencies require overhead projectors, and so on. We're not saying don't use these; we are saying be really sure you need them.

- Tests and questionnaires can sometimes be boring to complete and in the end induce that devastating question abhorred by all trainers but so necessary to keep us on our pedagogical toes—"So what?"

- Flip charts are a permanent record; can be used in a hundred different ways by you and participants for artwork, structured exercises, brainstorm recording devices, and so forth.

- Chalkboards are messy, and things get wiped off.

- Never be without your masking tape!

- Name tags sometimes look a bit formal, but they are invaluable for climate building. We even ask people who all know one another to wear tags, at least on the first day, to help us out. We can then refer to them by name, which is essential to good climate building (page 30).

- Notebooks or paper must be provided with pens and pencils.

- Videotapes have the advantage over films in that they do not require lowered lights.

- A copying machine close by is an asset.

- Posters with humorous sayings or thought-provoking quotations can be fun and help set the climate, but they are also used to make a learning point. Many of the Argus posters are excellent for this (see chapter 9), but if they are not available, make your own.

- Handouts need updating. Also, don't be tempted to use a handout for one course that was specifically designed for another. The examples may not be relevant.

Choosing procedures and structures

The important factors to be considered in choosing procedures and structures are indicated by the following questions.

CAN YOU USE THE PROCEDURE AGAIN?

It is obviously more desirable if any procedure you develop is reusable. A videotape may be ideal for your purpose, but if you cannot see the likelihood of being able to use it again, is it really worth your time investment?

HOW MANY STAFF MEMBERS ARE REQUIRED?

Some procedures will automatically be ruled out if you do not have an adequate staff.

ARE THE PROCEDURES CONSISTENT WITH THE OBJECTIVES?

You don't run a course in participatory decision making in a highly autocratic way!

HOW MUCH TIME DOES THE PROCEDURE TAKE?

For program design, you need an accurate idea of how long a procedure takes. You can always gain time by making structural changes. For example, instead of getting people to share ideas in small groups, you put them into pairs or trios. Never program your course so highly that there is no opportunity for dealing with the unexpected.

How much space does the procedure require?

Small groups need a large room or a number of small rooms. Videotape recording equipment, if it is to be used for skills practice, is best situated in a room of its own to prevent participants from falling over cables. A circle arrangement involves considerably more space than do rows. You can always arrange for a double-layered circle. If you want to do small-group work, ensure that you do not find yourself, as we did on one occasion, in a banked lecture theater with built-in seating. All the participants could do was turn and talk to the persons next to them. After an experience like that, you learn to always check out your premises personally!

Is the procedure appropriate to its slot in the program?

Don't put passive procedures after lunch or dinner or at the beginning of the day. Lectures after a meal can be difficult even with the best lecturers. A film after lunch, in the dark, is an invitation to sleep.

Is the procedure appropriate for the participants/organization?

Seasoned participants used to highly active courses will be turned off by a program dominated by lectures. Inexperienced participants may be scared by highly experiential procedures. Encouraging participants, for example, to design their own learning experiences could create problems for them, their organization, and you if they work in an organization that permits little initiative or participation in decision making.

ORGANIZING THE PROGRAM

The design skill involved at this stage is that of sequencing, which we are now ready to discuss (Step 4). The first three steps below review what we have accomplished so far in the design process.

Step 1. We know our objectives and have analyzed our goals. (Goal Analysis Work Sheet, page 76.)

Step 2. We know the context in which the course will take place. (Context Profile, page 78.)

Step 3. We have selected which teaching procedures we would like to use (Teaching Procedures Checklist, page 88), which teaching structures we would like to use (Teaching Structures Checklist, page 94), and the materials we need (page 95.)

Step 4. We are ready to put the learning activities into a preferred sequence. There is no single best way to do this, and we find that the original sequence or schedule is nearly always adjusted before the program begins. Our suggestion for sequencing is as follows: (a) set down mealtimes and starting and closing hours for each day, (b) list learning outcomes in what seems to be a natural order (Is learning A prerequisite to learning B? Does it seem logical to learn X before Y?), (c) assign tentative time slots to each activity, (d) list at least two alternative teaching procedures for each outcome, (e) review this tentative schedule in regard to climate considerations, and (f) select the teaching procedure to be used and adjust the schedule accordingly.

A tentative schedule for the communications course example is used to illustrate steps a to d. Steps e and f are illustrated on page 106.

The actual process we used involved thinking first in terms of a three-hour morning period and a three-and-one-half-hour afternoon period and then designating more precise periods. Our initial listing did not include a review period at the end of the day; but after seeing the large amount of material we intended to cover, we deemed it wise to provide time for review and clarification.

Note that the procedures listed refer to specific items in our repertoire.

Step 5. Decide how much time can be slotted for each outcome, bearing in mind that some procedures can achieve multiple outcomes.

The choice of teaching procedures cannot be made in terms of pedagogic reasons alone. The vital element of the learning climate has to be considered.

TENTATIVE SCHEDULE DAY 1

TIME	OUTCOME	PROCEDURES
9:00–9:30	Climate building	Introduction exercise or triads exercise
9:30–10:00	Understand conflict definition	Lecturette, simulations, or case study
10:00–10:30	Climate building	Coffee, "meet three people" exercise, or nonstructured break
10:30–12:00	Understand and experience conflict-resolution procedure	Lecturette and simulation exercise, problem-solving groups, small groups or total group discussion
12:00–1:00	Climate building	Lunch
1:00–2:00	Understand perception, checking, and clarification skills	Demonstration, role playing, practice in trios
2:00–3:00	Understand probing skills	Film, demonstration, small-group practice
3:00–4:00	Understand application of communication skills to conflict-resolution	Case study, simulations, exercise
4:00–4:25	Review and clarification	Large group discussion, small groups, written questions, panel
4:25–4:30	Evaluation	Short form or open-ended statements

THE LEARNING CLIMATE

We are teaching people, not programming computers. Consequently, the complex varieties of human needs have to be considered in designing a course. Unless the socioemotional climate for participants and staff is right, the best-designed programs can fail.

Following is a list of the climate factors that have to be taken into account at this stage of our design. It outlines the climate factors that are important at each stage of producing a short-term training program, apart from actually conducting it, but only the design factors will be discussed. There is no separate mention of climate factors pertinent to the conducting phase, because chapter 6 delves into this fully, and the points are simply too numerous to list.

CLIMATE FACTORS

Contract Building

A clear understanding of the objectives.
A good working relationship with the contractor.
Direct or indirect communication with participants prior to the course.
Motivation of training staff.

Design

Built-in opportunity to check out the contract/expectations.
Possibility of renegotiating the contract.
Right mixture of participants.
Number of participants consistent with objectives.
Warm-up activities.
Introduction of training staff.
Built-in optimum rest time.
Possibility of lightening the climate.
Sequence of events to ensure a variety of training procedures and that sessions follow one another in terms of mood setting.

Development

Physical setting to help the climate.
Right timing of the course.
Staff relationships to enhance the climate.
Leader behavior to help create the right climate.
Catering arrangements to help the climate.
Inclusion of party.

Evaluation

Precourse evaluation.
Techniques for ongoing monitoring of the course.
End-of-course evaluation.
Postcourse evaluation.

BUILT-IN OPPORTUNITY TO CHECK OUT THE CONTRACT/EXPECTATIONS

We recommend always drawing up the contract in such a way that there is an opportunity during the first session to check it out together with expectations. Simply talking through the Contract Triangle (page 56) or brainstorming expectations, objectives, hopes, fears, and so on, will highlight this.

Trainer's Tip: Present your own objectives on a handout or flip chart.

POSSIBILITY OF RENEGOTIATING THE CONTRACT

Sometimes a contract cannot be negotiated again. So don't pretend that is possible if it isn't. In this case you are frequently checking for clarification, not for negotiation. It is often a good idea, if you have the leeway, to reserve a time slot that can be used to deal with issues and needs surfaced by the participants. You can also include a formal monitoring spot at the end of each day or session.

RIGHT MIXTURE OF PARTICIPANTS

Participants can vary greatly. In your design you will have to allow for differences in experience. If you have a choice, minimize this. Sometimes that is not possible, in which case it is vital that the design does not highlight a "them and us" situation.

If you are working with an organization, are there any problems due to status mix? We ran a course once organized by the personnel officer. He selected the participants. What he did not tell us was that there would be a promotion two weeks after the course and three of them were up for the same spot. Obviously, the entire group thought they had been put in the program to be specially observed and were totally uptight for the three-day course. The personnel officer had not foreseen the problem, especially as he was on good personal terms with each of them.

We have run highly successful courses with groups from all levels of a hierarchy. But you must *know* in advance and allow for inhibitions.

NUMBER OF PARTICIPANTS CONSISTENT WITH OBJECTIVES

If you have a design with skills practice in it, you need to ensure that there is an opportunity for everyone to practice. You are immediately into the numbers game.

Don't restrict your numbers automatically just because one part of the course demands individual attention for the participants. It is often possible to set the majority of participants at one task, while you work individually with others. This requires thinking through the activities involved and making sure that the group activity is something that participants can move in and out of easily. With careful planning, you can sometimes double the number of participants by a small increase in the staff.

Trainer's Tip: It is possible to do two things at once.

WARM-UP ACTIVITIES

When people come to a course, a great deal of energy is invested initially in fantasizing about fellow participants and the staff, wondering, and sometimes worrying, about what is to come and thinking about where they have just come from, what they are going to do about eating, or how they are getting home. With so much going on, people are unlikely to perceive much for the first few minutes; so make it a point not to launch straight into your program. On the contrary, you accept what is probably going on and design something that will help people let go of their "baggage" from outside and help them get to know one another. Examples are given in chapter 7.

INTRODUCTION OF TRAINING STAFF

We have already established that some fantasizing will be directed toward staff, so a form of introduction is called for. How you do this can set the mood for the whole course.

"Hello, I'm Dr. Hopson. What we are here to do today is . . ."

"Hello, welcome to this course on communications skills. I'm Barrie Hopson, and I'd like to communicate something about myself and how I got to sit in front of you this morning."

We feel strongly that introductions should not be left to chance. Put some real thought and imagination into planning those first few words.

BUILT-IN OPTIMUM REST TIME

A belief is prevalent among some trainers that participants must be kept working every minute of the day and then fall into bed exhausted at the end of the day.

Trainer's Tip: People stop learning when they are tired.

You will see that in the first day's course outlined on page 100, the afternoon session finished at 4:30. That enabled people to have a shower, rest, or drink before dinner. In fact, that first day looks very heavy. Some trainers like to start off with a fairly heavy first day and ease up later. Other trainers always like to have one free session, which might change each day (the day might have five sessions—two in the morning, two in the afternoon, and one in the evening).

The other danger is to give too much rest time. Participants can resent this. They might feel that the course could have been shorter, and they could be back at home or work sooner, or, in addition, that they are missing something that the staff might have to offer. It's not a bad idea to check out with them as part of an ongoing contract how much rest time they would like. Sometimes rest time can be presented as one option along with work options.

POSSIBILITY OF LIGHTENING THE CLIMATE

To lighten the climate is vital to many sessions. An intensive, heavy session is often best followed with one that is less demanding. In addition, training experiences can be made more or less enjoyable. It is not possible to have a fun session each time, but program planners should try to include fun elements wherever possible. If this is difficult to do during the sessions, perhaps something is possible outside of them—a party, games in the evening, exercises that may be remotely connected with the course outcomes but whose primary purpose is fun. The staff's own styles of behavior are vital here. Not everyone can impart humor to sessions. This is not necessary, but it is desirable to have at least one staff member with this ability.

SEQUENCE OF EVENTS

The main reasons for this step in the design phase are to ensure a variety of training procedures and that sessions follow one another in terms of mood setting.

The virtues of ensuring a variety of training procedures have already been expounded. Ensuring that sessions follow one another in terms of mood setting can be vital. Don't follow one emotionally demanding session with another. On the other hand, if people have had a heavy session, they might not be in the mood for something trivial. It is only by experience that you can predict this sort of thing in advance, and even then you will often be wrong. It is useful to have some alternatives for sessions with predictable question marks. For example, in one of our courses, we had just experienced a hilarious session playing a management game. There was a coffee break, during which everyone remained high as kites, followed by a talk from an invited speaker. The poor man never knew what hit him. He had a class of disruptive children who wanted to play games. Such a thing could have been anticipated by the trainers.

PROGRAM DEVELOPMENT WORK SHEET

TIME	OUTCOME	CONTENT	PROCEDURES/ STRUCTURES	MATERIALS
9:00–9:30	Know one person Everyone introduced to group	Participants and staff biodata	10 min. pairs 20 min. short introductions	Markers 3x5 cards
9:30–10:00	Understand conflict definition	Smith book pp. 30–49	20 min. case study Lecturette 10 min. question and answer	Case study handout
10:00–10:30	Get to know two more people	Not applicable	Coffee break—assign "Know two more people"	None
10:30–11:30	Understand and experience conflict-resolution procedure	L & H manuscript pp. 110–132	Conflict-resolution exercise (small groups)	Data sheets Reaction forms Overhead projector Transparencies
11:30–12:00	Clarification	Question and answer	Large-group discussion	Chalkboard
12:00–1:00			Lunch	
1:00–2:00	Understand perception, checking, and clarification skills	*Helping* chapter 4	15 min. demonstration Triad practice	Transparencies Overhead projector Handout

Time	Objective	Reading/Assignment	Activity	Materials
2:00–2:45	Understand probing skills	*Helping* chapter 4	Lecturette Probing exercise	Handout
2:45–3:00			Refreshments	
3:00–4:00	Understand application of communication skills to conflict-resolution problems	L & H manuscript pp. 20–35	Case study Conflict-resolution exercise	Handout Data sheet Film
4:00–4:25	Clarification	Question and answer	Large-group discussion	None
4:25–4:30	Evaluation		Individual	Form
4:30–6:00			Free time	
6:00–7:30			Dinner	
7:30–9:00	Climate building	Nonverbal communication exercise Paper	Nonverbal communication exercise	None

SETTING THE FINAL SEQUENCE

It is now time to look again at the design for the first day in terms of climate considerations. For this we introduce the Program Development Work Sheet (page 106).

This Program Development Work Sheet highlights the importance of climate building. The first thirty minutes are given over to it. All coffee breaks and mealtimes are opportunities for the staff to build or improve climate. The entire evening is devoted to light relief. There are ancillary learning gains, but the major benefit will be derived from the relationships developed in the groups, the shared experiences and jargon, and the fun evening that will be remembered. It would have overloaded participants anyway to have had another serious learning session after such a demanding day.

This first day of an actual course also illustrates the way procedures and structuring can be varied.

Design is hard work but can also be great fun. It should reflect the personalities of the staff, the needs of the participants, and the contract with the organization. It needs to be systematic, it is ongoing, and it is never truly over until the course ends.

We have devoted much space to the topic of design. We have also taken you through the process systematically, asking you to dot every *i* and cross every *t*. In practice, of course, it is rarely as neat. We are also aware that the more experienced you become, the less inclined you are to fill in checklists. However, we still find it invaluable to have the checklists around to remind us of things to do and to help generate alternatives. Experience has its drawbacks as well as its advantages. Confidence can breed sloppiness; continued success can encourage the belief that "we can always wing it." The experienced trainer, while developing a greater range of conducting skills to deal with problems "on the day," will never cut corners on the design stage. Life is simply easier that way!

6 Development Stage

When the design stage is complete, we have a set of specifications for the course. The next step is to get it off the drawing board and into the stage of developing materials, making physical arrangements, and hiring and training staff. Climate-building inputs and backup materials are developed, so that by the end of the development stage, there is only one thing left to do—run the course.

DEVELOPING THE LEARNING CLIMATE

The importance of a good learning climate was underlined in the previous chapter. People will not learn unless they want to learn. So how can we develop the program in such a way that they are desperate to join in and learn from it?

In the previous chapter we also listed climate-building factors at all stages except the ongoing conducting stage. In this chapter we will first be focusing on the six points mentioned under Development in Climate Factors.

Physical setting

How will the physical setting help the climate? In the final analysis, each trainer has to develop his or her own checklist, which will be determined by the trainer's own personality and the type of courses each runs. The following is ours.

PHYSICAL FACILITIES CHECKLIST

Will the building enhance or inhibit the learning climate?
What is the surrounding environment like?
Will the time of year make any difference?
What are the residential facilities like?
Any recreational facilities?
What are the lines of communication with the outside world?
How accessible is the place?
What technical/secretarial facilities are available?
Is there a room large enough for total group sessions?
Are there sufficient numbers of small group rooms?
What seating is available?
Are the heating, lighting, and ventilation adequate?
Is there freedom from distractions and interruptions?

Each of these items is important, and failure to consider them can have negative results for your program. Let's examine each briefly.

BUILDING APPROPRIATE FOR LEARNING CLIMATE

It must be questioned whether or not the building is suitable for the particular type of program. One of us used to run sensitivity training groups of two weeks' duration. For that, an out-of-the-way hotel was ideal. People felt cut off and that helped them focus on their own small world they were creating. Such a setting, however, would be disastrous for a serial-type course designed to bring engineers up to date on new air conditioning systems. The isolation and the excessive travel would be irritants.

If your building is a disaster, you will have to impose your personality on it. Try posters or flip charts with quotations. Failing that, you will need to plan to make an immediate impact on people when they arrive. Turn the negative into a positive.

SURROUNDING ENVIRONMENT

What is the surrounding environment like? Sometimes it's simply another room in the same building. Then the challenge is separating the training experience from the rest of the organization.

You may be in a beautiful rural setting, in which case use it! Participants can feel frustrated if they get no time to sample the delights awaiting them through the windows. If it is a residential course near places of aesthetic or historical interest, give them opportunities to visit.

TIME OF YEAR

Will the time of year make any difference? In midwinter in a place where snow is predictable, allow some leeway in your design for the starting time to ensure that you don't have a dribble of latecomers. At the height of summer, you might plan for your rest sessions to be largely in the afternoon; and if avoidable, don't arrange sessions in a glass classroom with no air conditioning in midsummer. These points may sound trivial, but they have happened and are likely to affect climate. Even if they cannot be avoided, being aware of them will help you control them or even use them to your advantage.

RESIDENTIAL FACILITIES

What are the residential facilities like? Always check. A group of women who came for a five-day course expected private rooms and were horrified to discover on arrival that they were in a dormitory. In some training centers it is necessary to bring along your own linen or towels. Find out. Are the toilet arrangements satisfactory? Are there sufficient bathrooms? Lining up for the bathroom, however short or long a time, does not get the day off to a good start!

RECREATIONAL FACILITIES

For residential courses a bar is a tremendous asset. In addition, if your center has facilities for any kind of sports, good jogging tracks, or country walks, or ready access to any of these, you are already in some participants' good books.

COMMUNICATION

What are the lines of communication with the outside world? Easy telephone and mail links are essential. But be careful about the telephone. We don't usually allow participants to receive calls during sessions. Consequently, we require a message-taking facility.

ACCESSIBILITY OF THE PLACE

Can you get to the place by car only? To have no public transportation facilities could create problems for some participants. Check this out.

TECHNICAL/SECRETARIAL FACILITIES

What technical/secretarial facilities are available? How many teaching aids that you require are on the premises? Overhead projectors, slide projectors, and even film projectors can usually be checked on over the telephone. Video systems, with their notorious lack of compatibility, are often a different story. In case of emergencies or brilliant moments of spontaneity, are there any typing facilities or at least a photocopying machine?

ROOM SIZES

Is there a room large enough for total group sessions? The room should not just be the right size but also the right shape. If you want a large circle, you don't want it broken up by half walls or pillars. Always judge room size according to the teaching structure you want to use. Can your large group split up into small working groups without sitting back to back?

ROOMS FOR SMALL GROUPS

Are there sufficient numbers of small group rooms? If there are not enough small rooms, can you compromise using your large room? Does the hotel or dormitory have any large bedrooms or even small ones that are available for small groups?

AVAILABILITY OF SEATING

Before deciding how long to ask people to sit passively, it is vital that you consider the type of seating you will find. Hard upright chairs for long periods are for masochists only. Soft armchairs encourage people to curl up and go to sleep. They also take up considerable space and make it difficult for participants to see one another. Having people seated at different heights can produce some strange dynamics. Unless the course is designed to investigate such phenomena, we suggest that all participants sit on similar chairs.

HEATING, LIGHTING, AND VENTILATION

Are the heating, lighting, and ventilation adequate? This is most important in summer and winter. If you have ever had to run a course in a room whose windows would not open, with central heating blasting away and the sun streaming unpredictably through the windows—it was only March—you will know what we mean! Try to get buildings or rooms whose heat can be controlled manually and whose windows can be opened—a decreasing luxury, it would seem.

DISTRACTIONS AND INTERRUPTIONS

Is there freedom from distractions and interruptions? Don't run a course next to a noisy concourse, a typing pool, or a busy street. If you are operating within a work organization, invest in huge signs that politely keep people out.

A more unusual type of distraction occurs when you are preoccupied with maintaining the physical setting. For example, we ran a course in a stately home whose curator was terrified lest we ravage the expensive murals and hand-painted wallpaper with our masking tape and magic markers. To us it seemed that the historical goodies were not worth the anxiety.

The same curator was eager to join in! This illustrates another possible distraction—nonparticipants who feel free to move into your course at will.

Timing

Is the timing of the course right? Not in one course we heard about. The entire sales team went on a four-day course on improved selling techniques. The trainers were unaware until the third day that over the next three weeks all the participants would undergo their evaluation interviews. Some of the performances were manic, to say the least.

In addition to checking out interesting happenings in the organization, carefully consult your diary for public holidays and major sporting events. For two consecutive years we planned weekend courses six months in advance, only to discover that our scheduled meetings clashed with the British soccer cup final—an event that empties the streets of Britain. The participants had to attend the courses, and we were very popular when we negotiated free time to coincide with the match. This is not universal, however. Sports haters resent having a piece of the course taken away simply to make room for a sporting event. Conclusion: Check out your calendar.

Trainer's Tip: Check to see what is happening in and out of the organization before you set the time for the course.

Staff relationships

Will staff relationships enhance the climate? What is one of the first things you notice when eating in a restaurant? For us it is the quality of the staff relationships. If they seem at ease with one another and even look as if they are enjoying one another's company, the food somehow tastes better. On the other hand, we have seen restaurants where the waiters were having such a good time joking, shouting, chatting, and hugging that the customers seemed to be irrelevant!

Trainer's Tip: Staff relationships are probably the biggest single predictor of a successful or unsuccessful course.

There is no worse experience than trying to run a course with a staff member you don't trust or whose competence is questionable. There are ways of checking a staffer in advance if you have not worked with someone before (page 158). The key factor in selecting your staff team should be the quality of the relationships. If the staff members trust one another, they can even make jokes at one another's expense. The effect on participants is to make them feel comfortable and trusting.

Trainer's Tip: If you have a problem with a colleague, tackle it immediately.

Don't go into a course with unresolved issues. This cannot help but affect the climate. Participants might base their behavior on the way staff members behave with one another.

Leader behavior and climate

How can leader behavior help create the right climate? The following list illustrates a variety of positive and negative contributions of leader behavior.

BEHAVIOR THAT CONTRIBUTES TO NEGATIVE CLIMATE	BEHAVIOR THAT CONTRIBUTES TO POSITIVE CLIMATE
Style of leadership is inappropriate, e.g., too democratic in a highly autocratic system, or vice versa.	Style of leadership is congruent with what the group is used to. Changes are introduced, but carefully.
Objectives obscure or not well communicated.	Objectives clear and clearly presented (preferably in writing).
Participants not given an opportunity to influence the contract, voice concerns or anxieties.	Participants are consulted— what is not negotiable is pointed out and explained; what is negotiable is made clear. Anxieties and concerns are elicited, listened to, and responded to.
Leader does not keep to agreed-upon contract.	Leader keeps to contract but is open to renegotiation if appropriate.
The procedure is not in keeping with objectives, e.g., the group is told of the importance of really listening to one another, but the leader does not listen to group members.	The procedure is consistent with the objectives.

BEHAVIOR THAT CONTRIBUTES TO NEGATIVE CLIMATE	BEHAVIOR THAT CONTRIBUTES TO POSITIVE CLIMATE
Leader does not keep group to the point. Irrelevancies pursued.	Group kept to the point unless they wish strongly to do something else, in which case the contract is renegotiated.
Individuals or small groups allowed to dominate.	Participation is evenly distributed by appropriate leadership behavior and by the use of exercises that give "air time" to everyone.
Conflict buried or ignored.	Conflict brought into the open and dealt with.
Leader not alert to the dynamics of the group or skilled enough to deal with the issues.	Leader has necessary observation and group management skills.
Overly serious or inappropriate humor.	Humor used to lighten the sessions.
No self-disclosure, so participants never know the person behind the role of leader.	Appropriate self-disclosure. The leader is seen as a real person with concerns, joys, and vulnerabilities like everyone else.
Low trust level. Participants feel the need to be defensive.	High trust level. The leader has used trust-building skills, e.g., appropriate self-disclosure, warmth, genuineness, accepting of differences, not being defensive when criticized.
Competitive attitude.	Cooperation and joint problem-solving approach. Climate set by leader's behavior.
Overcritical or attacking-type feedback.	Feedback given, constructively.

BEHAVIOR THAT CONTRIBUTES TO NEGATIVE CLIMATE	BEHAVIOR THAT CONTRIBUTES TO POSITIVE CLIMATE
Leadership behavior unpredictable. Participants never know what is coming next.	Leadership behavior predictable.
Leader relates especially to one or two participants.	Leader's relationships evenly distributed.
Specialist or jargon language.	Language appropriate to group, and safeguards built in, e.g., a jargon sheet, a flip chart put up especially for people to write jargon on as it occurs. Sheet used to illustrate that we all use jargon.
Group decisions not acted upon.	Action taken immediately on group decisions.
Leader never available at breaks and mealtimes.	Leader is available outside of sessions if any group participant is experiencing special difficulties.
Leaders never mix with participants. Disappear into exclusive staff groups.	Leaders distribute themselves at breaks and mealtimes. Staff sessions arranged for other times, e.g., immediately after lunch or at end of day.
Feelings not checked out. The leader makes assumptions about how participants feel.	Feelings are checked out during and between sessions.
Silence becomes threatening and creates awkwardness.	Silence used positively for thought and reflection.
Coleaders always sit next to one another, creating a very powerful front. This makes it more difficult to challenge.	Coleaders place themselves away from one another. This reduces the us/them feeling and also enables 360° monitoring of individual reactions.

BEHAVIOR THAT CONTRIBUTES TO NEGATIVE CLIMATE	BEHAVIOR THAT CONTRIBUTES TO POSITIVE CLIMATE
Coleaders never express differences in front of the group and never discuss design changes openly.	Coleaders discuss differences openly, thereby act as valuable role models. There has to be a high level of mutual trust and professional respect to do this. When appropriate, design changes are discussed in front of the group.
Leaders extend time of sessions and run over.	Agreed-upon time is always adhered to. Any changes occur only after thorough negotiation.

Catering arrangements

Will the catering arrangements help the climate? Flexible coffee and tea breaks are always desirable. Given the opportunity, make your own if necessaries are provided. This enables you to make changes depending on what is happening. Meals are often more difficult to move. Institutions have their own programs to keep.

We find it a useful practice to spend time with the cook or catering manager before a course starts. If you overrun your schedule slightly, there will be less chance of participants' having their meals slammed down in front of them.

We never encourage large lunches with alcoholic beverages. Our suggestion is either a light lunch or a buffet, which has the added advantage of people mixing together over the salad bowls!

Trainer's Tip: Try to get all participants to eat together.

Try to ensure that some do not go out to eat while others stay in, or that they all drift off to different places. Eating together has great social significance in most cultures; for example, the institution of the dinner party in middle-class Western cultures. It helps make participants more cohesive.

We have sometimes used the idea of a "course feast." Typically, we have asked people to bring food and drink on the last day to contribute to a feast. The idea is to bring something that will be somewhat special to the group. (Be careful not to create a cordon bleu contest.) It is essential that trainers share in bringing the food.

We occasionally set tasks for people to do over a meal—"Sit next to someone you haven't talked to yet"; "Share your reactions to the morning with the people at your table." Sometimes we've even set structured questions on the tables for people to pursue over the meal. On the whole, though, we believe that meals are for enjoying, relaxing, and getting to know one another.

If there are no eating facilities on the premises, it will be appreciated if you produce a handout listing nearby eating places, together with information on how to get there, the type of food served, and the price range.

Parties

Will there be a party? This question is not just meant literally. It refers to the fact that participants and staff often feel the need to mark the end of a learning experience, especially in residential and longish serial courses. We have organized parties or, even better, allowed and sometimes encouraged participants to organize them. We have invited everyone to a glass of wine or sherry at the end of a day's course. We have all gone out for a meal somewhere—sometimes making it more of a social experience by inviting spouses. Making an event of the end of a course helps people "close" it psychologically for themselves. There are often attacks of "reunionitis," but these are usually subject to spontaneous remission.

Trainer's Tip: Don't forget to plan your closing as carefully as every other part of the course.

THE IDEAL LEARNING CLIMATE

What is the ideal learning climate? There isn't one. We are not trying to prescribe any particular climate, though obviously our biases show through. What we are emphasizing is that a good learning climate does not happen by chance, even if it sometimes appears that way—especially to the participants. It has to be planned for as systematically and cold-bloodedly as everything else.

Trainer's Tip: A *good learning climate will enhance good teaching procedures and will compensate for poor teaching procedures.*

PROCEDURES AND MATERIALS

In chapter 5 the teaching procedures were chosen in theory, staff members were hired in theory, and materials were earmarked on paper. These now have to be translated into action plans.

Hiring staff

Your first priority is to hire your staff. Ideally, staff should be in on the initial design. Often this is not possible. Sometimes it is not even necessary; for example, when you are hiring someone for one particular spot on the program. We suggest the following procedure for hiring and orienting staff.

- Follow your own rules of contracting (chapter 4). Give information on what the contractor wants, the scope of the training, the participants, the type of organization, and who controls what. In other words, inform potential staff.

- Offer a fee and expenses. State clearly whether any negotiation is possible.

- Know that dates are confirmed and planning meetings arranged.

- Check on transportation.

- Put your contract with each staff member in writing, for the same reasons that you put agreements with your contractor in writing (page 52).

Developing procedures and materials

Your first staff meeting will involve showing the design to date or even beginning the design. The next stage is to work out who is doing what. For an example, we shall continue with the Program Development Work Sheet on page 106.

Step 1. What has to be developed, what is already in existence? Using the Program Development Work Sheet for the first day of the communications skills course, look at the last two columns, headed Procedures/Structures and Materials, respectively. Make a list of all the procedures materials (including lecture notes) that will be used. Before deciding who is to take responsibility for developing these, you need to list the remaining staff work load, again indicating what has been and needs to be done. This will differ from course to course. We are continuing with our example. Dates are given for each item. Remember, films and books take time to order, and handouts take time to prepare and write. These jobs need to be ranked in time sequence.

ITEM	DONE	TO BE DONE	WHEN
Checking out premises.	X		May 10
Seeing motel manager and catering manager and explaining course.	X		May 10
Hiring video equipment.		X	May 12
Visiting manager-director and working through the course design.		X	May 15
Letter to participants.		X	May 16
Checking on existing handouts (enough for all participants).		X	May 20
Organizing other teaching materials into a material box.		X	June 1

Step 2. Who is to do what preparation? With these two lists it is now possible for the work to be divided. We usually like to work out a "preference run-through" first. Asking everyone to state preferences takes care of many items without contention. The

remainder can then be negotiated and initials put by each.

Step 3. Who does what on the program? A preference run-through is a gc ɔd idea here, too. However democratically, programs are designed and decisions are made. We would recommend that there be one person with overall responsibility, whether that person be designated director, leader, or coordinator. That person is probably the best person to start off a course because the message regarding who is in overall control is then passed on to the participants.

AVOIDING ADMINISTRATIVE PROBLEMS

Control is essential for success. Even if the control is shared or passed around, at any moment anyone in a course—trainer or participant—should know who is responsible for what is happening at that time. This is your number one guideline for avoiding administrative problems. Your second guideline is to try to anticipate as much as possible in advance. If you have worked through all the checklists in the last three chapters, very little should have slipped through the net by this stage. Administrative problems usually revolve around someone's not receiving important information, somebody's acting unilaterally, or responsibilities not being carefully defined, designated, and checked out.

Trainer's Tip: Make yourself a materials box.

A materials box can vary, depending on what is to be contained in it. We use a cardboard box with sections—one section for videotapes, another for the ring binder that contains overhead transparencies. Always taped to the lid is a course checklist, which we can go through when filling the box. We have specific course-related items like handouts, as well as general items for any course.

FAIL-SAFE PROGRAMS

Can a program be fail-safe? In a word—never! However, there

are a number of things you can do. You should always have the following:

- Alternative staff in mind in case someone drops out.
- Backup material developed in case such things as films and videotapes do not show up, or in case electrical equipment breaks down.
- Extra sets of materials—participants will lose some even if you don't.
- Strategies ready should equipment break down.

Trainers Tip: Always ask yourself, What's the worst thing that can happen?—and plan for it.

It probably will not be disastrous anyway. We have had many examples of disasters that have been turned into positives. One involved an interviewing procedures course with three video systems during a power workers' strike. Without warning, the equipment and lighting would be immobilized for three-to-four-hour periods. We took with us battery-powered tape recorders and candles. It was the most romantic course we ever ran. Another disaster was running a course for salesmen on telephone selling when a storm cut off all the telephone lines! We did some marvelous simulation sessions instead. Climate, we find, can improve as a result of disasters. The participants feel sorry for you and will try to help, and the challenge seems to bind people together more as a group.

You have now anticipated and planned for every possibility. You have made all your physical and administrative arrangements, developed all your procedures and materials, and hired, oriented, and trained your staff. There now remains one job to do—conduct the program.

7 Conducting the Program

After all the effort expended in designing and developing your short-term training program, the day of truth finally arrives. You've actually got to conduct the thing! Speculations, daydreams, and idealizations must be put aside and the reality of encountering live participants faced. Many experienced instructors still feel a few stomach butterflies when they begin workshops or seminars. We certainly do and view it as a good sign. In every program you produce, you put yourself on the line. There are many similarities between teaching and performing on the theatrical and musical stages. Unless you can maintain your audience's attention and develop their interest in what is happening, it is impossible to carry on. And that is a challenge. Even the best-planned program depends upon an instructor for delivery.

Directing a short-term training program can be a very challenging, exciting, and rewarding experience. In complex programs, the director may feel like a Chinese juggler balancing eighteen plates and balls at once. The key is to perform the directing function so that it is hardly noticeable. A really well produced program seems to flow naturally, with highs and lows timed favorably. Participants move from activity to activity with only minimal direction, and a positive feeling prevails. Participants feel they're part of the program, see its relevance, and are confident about raising questions and making suggestions. There is also clarity about what is happening. Participants and instructors

124

understand one another and share a common purpose. The we-they feeling is absent or at least not important. When all this is present, you have a healthy learning climate. Or to view the situation from the instructor's perspective, the healthy climate allows you to teach effectively—to use the materials and procedures you have developed. Without a healthy learning climate, both participant and instructor are handicapped.

Consequently, as we examine the process of conducting short-term training, we have a twin focus. The first is instruction—using your instructional materials and procedures. The second is building climate. In reality, these two functions overlap. Effective instruction contributes to a healthy climate, and climate-building efforts motivate participants to learn.

While not discounting the importance of having effective instructional procedures and materials, we want to emphasize both the importance and the subtleness of climate building. We have already noted many things you can do to build good climates prior to conducting programs. In addition to these efforts, nearly everything you do during the program can influence climate. The way you dress, your manner of responding to questions, the use of first or last names, your nonclass behavior (for instance, where you eat and drink, and with whom), and your own physical and mental conditions all can have significant impact on climate. That is one reason why many effective instructors find conducting short-term training programs very demanding and exhausting. When you are aware of your almost constant potential impact on climate and use the many opportunities to contribute to it, you are performing at a very high level. You are constantly alert.

Effective instructors of many short-term programs, in other words, are constantly "up." Obviously, this varies with the program design, content, and procedures. But even in the most straightforward short-term training program, the instructor is the key to building good climate. There are always opportunities to be encouraging, pleasant, and appreciative of participant concerns. For example, such acts as being alert to room temperature and lighting and keeping these at comfortable levels can do much for the learning climate.

And, finally, as we shall see, you must pay attention to your own satisfactions as an instructor. If instructors are the key to good climate, they must perceive their efforts as effective. You, as well as the participants, must receive payoffs in order for short-term training programs to achieve their purposes.

In concentrating on the actual conducting of short-term training programs, this chapter at times deals with issues and topics discussed in previous chapters. In such instances our perspective is now an operational one, as compared with the earlier views of design and development.

KEEPING YOUR SANITY

Throughout, this book has emphasized the special features of short-term training, particularly the high rewards that can be obtained but also the extra pressures that the staff face. The intensity and pace of running the program make it a very demanding activity. So how does one avoid trainer burnout? The key is to maintain both psychological and physical health. If you are physically healthy, you are better equipped to remain psychologically healthy.

Physical health

Enough has been written recently about the importance of physical fitness to overall health. With roads packed with joggers, perhaps it seems redundant to raise the issue again. We do so because in our experience many trainers regard track suits as status symbols for the wardrobe and not for the track. Simply possessing one convinces its owner that he or she is deriving from it the benefits of exercise.

We would point out that as a trainer you need to stay physically fit for two reasons: (1) to prevent trainer burnout and (2) for the good of your participants. In an extremely important research study (*Kids Don't Learn from People They Don't Like*),* Aspy and Roebuck stated the behavior characteristics that differentiated

---

* David Aspy and Flora Roebuck. *Kids Don't Learn from People They Don't Like*. Amherst, Mass.: Human Resource Development Press, 1977.

"good" teachers from "poor" ones. The good teachers were those who were able to demonstrate respect, who were genuine and real with their students, and who showed that they could empathize with their students' problems. Respect, genuineness, and empathy —the same relationship skills that distinguish between effective and less effective counselors and therapists. They discovered one other characteristic, however, which is of particular interest to us here. Those teachers who were rated high on these interpersonal skills were also rated high on one other dimension—physical fitness. Not surprising when you think about it. If you're tired, you are likely to be more irritable, more judgmental, less likely to look at a problem situation as a problem than as an attack on your authority. Good teachers move about a lot. They inject energy into the teaching situation.

Up until this point, we have been emphasizing the importance of remaining physically fit generally. Let us now look at life in courses in particular. A subject like physical health must really remain a matter of finding your own salvation. However, we shall share some of our lifesavers with you.

☐ At the end of an afternoon, for example, before dinner, with an evening session to come, go running or take a swim instead of pouring alcohol into an already tired body.

☐ After lunch take a walk. Have your staff meeting on a walk.

☐ Go through a personal exercise program when you have a free spot during the day. Certainly try to keep it up at the end or at the beginning of a training day. Often you will not feel like doing it, but one of the pleasant consequences of an exercise program is that although you may feel emotionally drained and physically exhausted beforehand, you will actually feel more energized and more mentally alert after a ten-minute workout.

☐ Diet is an important factor. If you train regularly, and especially if many of your courses are residential, you are often faced with the offer of three large meals a day and quantities of alcohol, and you spend a great deal of time sitting. Exercise can help to some extent, but it is vital that you regulate your diet. Have a salad for lunch instead of a three-course de-energizer and calorie raiser. In fact, protect your participants from such lunches. Not only are they bad for them healthwise but also are conducive to a sleepy postlunch session.

☐ We often take bags of fresh fruit with us, as you can live for days in some hotels without ever seeing food in its natural state.

Psychological health

The first step to psychological health is physical fitness. But what about after that? Again, we can offer only a range of tips as a starter. You will know yourself best.

☐ In residential courses, leave all home and work maintenance behind. Don't try to plan your next program in free slots. You need that time to relax.

☐ Relax. Lie down for ten minutes during the day and do some progressive relaxation or yoga deep breathing. If you meditate, this will do the trick.

☐ Give yourself a treat occasionally. Have a massage or a sauna at the end of the day. Have a special drink, watch a favorite television show, and so on.

☐ If you are running a nonresidential course, plan for the kind of evening you need to relax. For some people that is arranging to do nothing; for some it's meeting with good friends.

☐ Don't overload. Don't run one course during the day and another one in the evening.

Trainer's Tip: You must give yourself high priority.

☐ Don't change your whole design at the last minute, however brilliant your new idea is. You'll give everybody a heart attack— including yourself.

☐ Work out how you can best relax before starting a course. One trainer we know likes to lie down for twenty to thirty minutes before a course starts. Another simply refuses to talk. Another disappears to the bathroom for solitude.

☐ Have your travel arrangements organized to minimize hassle. Double-check train or flight times. Make sure your car is working. Allow plenty of time.

☐ Don't skimp to save money. Consider a taxi instead of the airport bus. Pay a dollar or two to have your bags carried.

☐ Use your colleagues to maintain your sanity. One value of working with other people is the "discharge factor." We have often maintained our cool only by blowing it to each other. After a particularly harrowing session, in which, for example, you have had to deal with an especially difficult participant, the sheer joy of being able to bad-mouth the individual to your colleagues is unparalleled! After the discharge you can reenter, smiling, able to cope anew. There's nothing cynical about this. The problem has as much to do with you as with the disrupter anyway, so why should he or she receive all the flak, especially if it could sour the climate for everyone? Discharge the anger from your system, and you will be freer to deal with the problem.

☐ Protect yourself from participants. There are times when you can feel that you have been set upon by vampires. It's often difficult to say no to keenness and enthusiasm, but participants don't always realize that what is free time for them can be work for you. For example, after having worked during the morning, you sit down for lunch, and participants pick your brains, discuss their problems, argue with you, and so on. You are working again in the afternoon. They rush more questions at you during the coffee break. They offer to buy you a drink before dinner so that they can pump you some more and sit next to you at dinner. At the end of the evening session, you are confronted again, and as midnight approaches and the alcohol is settling, you have people who want you to listen to their life stories, work out a new computer system for them, or test out an idea. STOP. An essential survival skill is knowing when and how to say no. Unless you can take that kind of thing in your stride for the sake of the rest of the course, you need to protect yourself. You might even be open about this at some point in the course. This depends so much on the kind of person you are. Some trainers are such prima donnas that they should never be let loose with any training staff. Others simply have a preference for being totally able to do their own thing, but unless a person is a devout loner, he or she can find working with good colleagues one of the most significant ways of reducing stress.

Coleadership

In the above paragraphs, we alluded to the advantage of having a partner to "blow your top" to when things become too rough. Let's explore the overall advantages of having two coequal leaders. We also look at the disadvantages in order to give both perspectives. These ideas may help you decide how you personally can function the best.

ADVANTAGES

- More time in preparation helps ensure common objectives and methods of working.

- Access to more resources—ideas, skills, information, experience.

- Feedback on performance.

- Shared work load.

- A broader range of strengths and weaknesses.

- One leader can conduct a group session, with the other following through, or can make points that the first leader has forgotten or pick up group behavior that the first leader has missed.

- The relationship can help build a warm, positive climate.

- Greater possibilities for humor—one leader can "bounce" off the other.

- Modeling—you have an opportunity to demonstrate how conflict can be dealt with in a constructive way, how to negotiate, compromise, and make decisions, and how changing the direction of a group or course openly as a result of developments can be of value.

- One can "carry" the other in case of an off-day, headache, or other problems.

- If one leader is in difficulty in a session, the other can step in.

- You can discharge stress and bad feelings to someone who will listen supportively.

- Input style can be varied. One person cannot appeal to everyone. Having two or more leaders increases the range of alternatives available, for example, sex, age, personality, voice types.

- By careful seating, two leaders should be able to pick up most things that are happening in a group. One leader cannot focus on everyone simultaneously.

- In case of administrative hassles, equipment breakdown, and such things, one person is free to deal with them.

DISADVANTAGES

- More time spent in preparation.

- Individual differences between coleaders can be so great that they are not on the same wavelength. This can lead to divisiveness, competition, and destructive conflict.

- Feedback to each other can be destructive if you do not respect and trust your coleader.

- A poor relationship will produce a poor group climate.

- Danger of in-jokes between the leaders, which can exclude the group.

- With insufficient trust, another leader might inhibit your style.

- Less autonomy.

- Can be distracting to have two leaders in the same room.

- Leaders sometimes talk to each other in group sessions instead of focusing attention—eye contact, as an example—on the group.

- Leaders can behave exclusively—taking coffee or eating apart from the group.

FINAL COUNTDOWN

We recommend two countdowns—before leaving for the course and on arrival. Have a checklist to go through before you leave. From your program design, you will have developed a list of materials and equipment you need to take. Check them off. Go through your materials box or suitcase. Check travel arrangements.

On arrival, again check the materials you have brought with you. In addition:

Check that all your equipment works.

Check that all coffee and tea breaks and mealtimes are scheduled as planned.

See that all rooms are furnished as they should be.

Contact the key people on site, renew your relationship with them, or if you have not met before, create a relationship with them.

If there is more than one trainer, ensure that one of them is responsible for making initial contact with participants as they arrive.

Following is a list of possible items for reviewing prior to the first encounter (described later). You will want to know where to find the items now that you have arranged for them. Your actual list, of course, will depend upon the nature of your program.

Utilities
    Electrical outlets
    Lavatories
    Drinking water
    Coffee maker

Equipment
    Projectors
    Extra projector bulbs
    Screens
    Television cameras
    Television recorder
    Television monitors

Television tapes
Audio recorders
Audiotapes
Flip charts
Special demonstrators
Computer terminal
Calculator
Hammer
Screwdrivers
Pliers
Alarm clock
Camera
Stapler
Pencil sharpener

Materials
Handouts
Films
Slides
Transparencies
Signs
Posters
Labels
Paper
Pens
Tape
Books
Pins
Folders
Carbon paper
Glue
Chalk

Administrative
Participant rooms
Fee arrangements
Telephone
Mail
Meals

Coffee breaks
Payment arrangements
Reimbursements
Special functions
Participant names, addresses, and phone numbers
Facility rules and policies
Certificate of attendance
Registration materials

Transportation
Local schedules
Pickup commitments
Special arrangements
Parking permits

Personnel
Clerical
Technical
Janitor
Room service

Other
Coffee, tea, etc.
Paper towels
Tissues
Aspirin
Band-Aids

FIRST ENCOUNTER

While the first official encounter with the participants of a short-term training program is usually the opening session, your contact with them may come earlier. In residential programs it may be the evening before the first session, and in most programs there is an exchange of correspondence prior to the programs. Consequently, there are a number of things that you can do prior to the program to begin climate building. And certainly what you do during the first sixty minutes of the program will establish a basic climate—one that may be difficult to change. Let's look at some ideas for maximizing the benefits from the first encounter.

Written material

Preprogram brochures, application forms, letters, and other printed material are your first introduction to the participants. Given no other information, this is what will determine their initial impression. So put some thought and effort into what you say and how it looks. An application form that is confusing, complicated, or unnecessarily long doesn't win friends.

Whenever possible, the written material that reaches participants should reinforce their desire to attend the program. It should be information that will be useful to them. Try to distinguish between what *you* want to put in a brochure and what *they* will find useful. There is often a difference. For example, is it really useful to list all the staff members in a brochure when participants won't recognize any of them? Probably not. It will simply take up space. Now, if certain staff members have credentials or experiences that will contribute to the learning climate by heightening participant enthusiasm, that's another matter.

One procedure we find useful is to read the brochure, bulletin, or announcement copy and then ask ourselves about each item: (1) How will that be useful to the participants and (2) How will it affect climate? If we can't give a positive answer to at least one question, we omit the item.

Another suggestion is to prepare or at least approve copy that is to be used in announcements, news releases, and other documents. Make sure that what participants are being told is true and that the impressions being created are consistent with your intentions. Such procedures as circulating a list of participants' names to them prior to the program, preparing preprinted name tags, and distributing kits that contain pencil, pad, and information about local cultural and recreational activities can all contribute to a positive first encounter.

If you are successful in this preprogram aspect of the first encounter, participants will have two positive reactions—"They've made a special effort" and "It's nice they recognize me personally."

Trainer's Tip: It matters not so much what you do but that you do something special.

Time schedule

The time schedule is a basic document. Adhere to it if you have developed it carefully. Punctuality is important if you want your program to progress as planned. With the exception of late arrivals, you begin the program having control over punctuality. As soon as you begin, you can lose control quickly. There are two ways to maintain control of the time schedule. The first is to model the behavior you want from participants. Arrive at sessions early. Allow plenty of time for setting up and for small talk. Then begin on time.

The second way of controlling your time schedule is to openly state your intentions. Somewhere in the orientation session, you can say something to the effect that "We like to start on time. Please allow yourself plenty of time to get settled before each session because we will stick to our schedule."

Controlling refreshment breaks can be a particularly annoying problem. There are ways of getting participants to return on time. For example, instructors of a twelve-hour intensive course in photography always announced unusual coffee break lengths. Never ten, fifteen, or twenty minutes but instead, "Okay, let's break nine minutes for coffee." Precisely nine minutes later they resumed their presentation. Participants learned immediately that the time periods were not approximations!

Trainer's Tip: Good timekeeping begins with you.

Rarely do we offer to negotiate changes in the schedule. But occasionally participants will ask for changes. These requests should be discussed for two reasons. First, it demonstrates your interest in the concerns of the participants and thus can contribute to climate. Second, they may have suggestions that will strengthen the program. For example, assume we've scheduled a one-hour lunch period for a workshop away from home. A local participant points out that there are few restaurants nearby, and thus any time allotment of less than one and one-half hours is inadequate. If this is correct, a schedule change would be appropriate. (We could, of course, have checked out the food situation when designing the program.)

In contrast, a request by a few members to start and stop an hour later than planned because of the distance they are commuting would normally not be sufficient reason for changing the schedule. These few knew about this when they agreed to attend, so why inconvenience the rest of the participants? However, if the others don't care, and it makes no difference to you, a change might be made in the interest of climate.

Establishing contact

Just prior to the first meeting can be an important aspect of your program in regard to climate. Many participants are alone and unsure of what to do. Rather than let them float about, provide opportunities for them to make contacts. One procedure is for staff members to move around introducing participants to one another. Another, which we find useful, is for a staff member to greet each participant as he or she arrives, provide each with a name tag, and then say, "We're really glad you're here, and we're eager for you to get to know other participants. Thus your assignment is that between now and the time our first session starts, you should meet and talk with five people you don't know. You and I have met, so you have only four to go." It usually works. You give people something to do while waiting to begin. Most of them want to meet others, and you've made it an official assignment.

The first physical meeting of the group is a time for demonstrating your ability, self-confidence, and concern for the group. Earlier we recommended some kind of warm-up or ice-breaking activity even in the most straightforward, technical short-term training programs. For example, even in a one-hour demonstration or orientation program, it can be useful for each participant to talk with a classmate for three to five minutes during the first ten minutes of the program. It is a means of relieving anxiety and tension, learning that they are not alone in their concerns, or simply establishing contact with another person and making the situation a little less impersonal. In larger programs twenty to thirty minutes spent in a warm-up activity can build rapport and create a climate that would take hours to develop without specific attention to climate.

There are hundreds of activities that can be used as warm-up exercises. What to do depends upon the nature and background of the group. Illustrative exercises are described below, and you will be able to modify these and develop others. (See also chapter 8.) Keep one basic idea in mind regarding a warm-up activity. Your purpose is to help people build relationships and a climate that will facilitate their learning. Don't try to teach program content in the warm-up activity. It simply confuses the issue.

It can be useful, however, to structure the warm-up exercise in relation to a particular concern or perception you have regarding the group. For example, if you perceive anxiety about the difficulty of the material, build the exercise so that it deals with that. If you believe there are many resistant participants, focus on that. If the group membership is heterogeneous, you may want to structure the exercise so as to bring out commonalities, such as sharing important high school memories. When you have no particular concerns, it can be useful to try a new twist to an exercise you have used before. Here are some examples of warm-up exercises that we find useful.

Distribute five-by-eight-inch cards and ask the participants to write three interesting facts about themselves. Form groups of three and have the members of each group exchange cards. Let each person be questioned by the other two regarding his or her facts.

Form pairs. Allow ten to fifteen minutes for pairs to prepare introductions of partners. The task is to make an informative and interesting introduction of one's partner to the group. Then proceed with the introductions.

Distribute a piece of paper to each participant. Instruct the participants to consider themselves as resources for the group and to note three or four contributions each that he or she might make during the training session. Give them a short period of time to wander about and read one another's sheets without talking. Then allow ten to fifteen minutes for following up with questions and conversation.

In total group, have each participant select a stranger and introduce himself or herself as of ten years ago. The stranger does likewise. In five to fifteen minutes, interrupt and have each participant repeat the process with another stranger—this time as of five years ago. Repeat as of now and as of five years in the future.

In addition to warm-up exercises, simply be alert and sensitive to the feelings that may exist. Everyday consideration of social interaction is usually sufficient, but this seems difficult for some trainers. We once participated in a workshop whose featured speaker, a world-famous figure in his field, was not a glib conversationalist. The kindest comment that can be made is that he was difficult to talk with. Those responsible for the program soon discovered this, as did others in the group, and the fellow was left standing by himself. Given this presession registration-coffee period with twenty-five minutes remaining before the program, the situation could have become uncomfortable. Fortunately, the spouse of one of the program leaders observed what was happening and assigned herself hostess responsibilities for the speaker. She introduced herself to him and then moved through the group introducing the man to the participants, all of whom, incidentally, were eager and honored for a moment with the great man. He, of course, got nothing but positive strokes. The social distance between him and his audience was decreased, which enhanced the climate for his presentation. Another solution would have been for the program chairperson to recognize that he was not good at making informal conversation and to provide for someone with this ability to host the speaker.

It is relatively easy for those conducting programs to help participants overcome social isolation. This is not to suggest that every participant needs a social director. Some may be content being by themselves with minimal contact with other participants. Our suggestion is for you to at least give the isolates opportunities to make contact. If they reject your effort, fine. Our experience, however, is that very few participants really want to remain isolated from the group.

Group norms

The initial encounter is also the time to establish the level of formality between staff and participants. In short-term training programs that last more than a few hours, norms that guide staff-participant interaction will develop quickly. These norms are informal rules for guiding people's behavior.

Trainer's Tip: Group norms don't just happen—they are made.

Why would you want to influence norms? Why not just let them develop naturally? There are two reasons, basically. The first is that group norms influence learning climate, and we have acknowledged that climate affects learning behavior. Thus, creating certain kinds of norms will encourage certain kinds of behavior. Consider, for example, a workshop for which you anticipate a wide variability in participant ability and experience. Some will be proficient and view the experience as a review. Others will be relatively uninformed and will have to struggle with some of the material. You decide to capitalize on the expertise in the group by using the better informed as tutors to the novices. To do this you want to create a very informal climate in which people feel free to ask for and give assistance to one another. You don't want to inhibit the process by having all the communication routed through you. In contrast, imagine a short-term training program at the conclusion of which 50 percent of the participants will be selected for promotions. In addition to their achieving the learning goals of the program, competition is an important factor. Participants will be selected for the new positions on the basis of a final examination and the training staff's ratings. In this situation, while you want a supportive, positive climate, you also want to avoid the camaraderie of the previous example.

The second reason for wanting to influence the level of formality is the kind of ongoing relationship you have with participants. In programs that require you to make significant judgments regarding participant performances, you may want a more formal relationship than in programs that do not require your evaluation of participants. It is not unusual for some participants to confuse an informal manner on the part of an instructor with a positive response to their performance. Should they subsequently receive a negative performance report, they may feel misled. When the instructor-participant relationship continues after the short-term training program, a relatively formal relationship may be appropriate. If, for example, you will supervise participants as employees following the workshop, an informal relationship during training may inhibit the supervision required later. At least a transition may be required from a nonsupervisory to a supervisory relationship, which some participants may find confusing.

In any event, think through the matter of level of relationship formality and determine what difference it makes to you. In our experience, more often than not, it is useful to influence the level of formality.

Establishing norms

How can you establish group norms? By both actions and words. The obvious unstated means of establishing the level of formality is through your own behavior. You and the other staff members set examples. The manner in which you dress sets a level of formality. There are exceptions, of course, but, generally speaking, if instructors dress up, so will participants. A group of people always dressed up offers a reminder that they are in a serious, business as usual, situation. A group in which the staff and the participants are less formally attired acknowledges greater equality.

The way in which the staff members talk to each other and the participants also influences the formality of relationships. If we are Barrie and Jack, the participants read the situation as informal. If we refer to each other as Mr. or Dr., they get a different message. Use first names if you want informality, Mr. and Ms. to encourage formality.

Even the initial arrangement of the group within the room influences the level of formality. A first encounter in which people are lined in rows, at desks or tables, looking into backs of heads, is less likely to be open and informal than one in which people sit in a circle. Placing a table or podium between you and your group makes you seem less one of them than if you joined their circle. Standing while they sit puts the level of formality some-where in between.

The first coffee break and meal also provide covert means of setting the relationship level. Joining the group for meals and cir-culating during coffee breaks move you closer to them. Isolating yourself during these times, or using them to prepare for the next session, seems to reinforce the differences between you and the participants.

How about a more open approach to establishing the level of formality? You simply discuss the issue. Identify any concerns and indicate the level of formality you want to exist. It is important that your own behavior be consistent with what you claim to desire, but an open discussion can speed up the process. Say, for example, "I'm Mary, and this is Bob. Let's use first names while we're together," or "Please come to us with any questions. We'll be joining you for coffee and meals, but in order to plan and review, the staff will go off by itself sometimes. We're not being antisocial—we just need to do some coordination from time to time."

To reiterate, if you want to influence the formality of relation-ships, you must do something about it. If you're unsure about your participants' perceptions and attitudes toward the short-term train-ing program, or think that there may be some negative aspects, why not precede the first encounter with refreshments? A small cost for a very effective demonstration of your concern for their comfort.

And remember, somewhere during the first encounter, check out your contract with the participants. What do they expect to gain from the short-term training program, and what do you and your staff expect to provide? If the two are not congruent, you have a basis for serious problems. Their frustration will grow as they invest more time and energy and gain less of what they anticipated, and yours will mount as they become less cooperative and enthusiastic.

KEY PEOPLE AND PHYSICAL FACILITIES

The physical facilities and the people who are the key to their operation can be extremely important factors in producing effective short-term training programs. Strange, then, that physical facilities and key people often get so little attention. Most of us would not hold a wedding reception in a barn, cook a gourmet meal for eight on a hot plate, or hold an important business luncheon at the local fast-food place. Yet trainers often produce programs in physical environments that are not congenial, and even detrimental, to their purposes. Poorly lighted basement motel rooms, cluttered public school classrooms, noisy conference rooms, and abandoned resorts come to mind. And the insensitivity to the importance of such people as custodians and secretaries would be humorous if not of such consequence.

The importance of physical facilities has been noted several times during the discussions of design and development procedures. Checklists can be used to help assure that facilities and arrangements meet your specifications. In spite of careful preparation, however, it is wise to give specific attention to physical facilities and key people during the conducting of programs. Here are several suggestions. What you actually do, of course, depends upon the nature of your program and the conditions and people involved.

- Make or renew contact with the people who actually operate the facilities and with those on whom you will depend for clerical assistance. Let them know that their help is important to you and that you are depending upon them. One means of establishing good rapport is to introduce these people to other staff members and the participants.

- Provide key people with a copy of your time schedule. Make notations regarding services you will need from them. Make sure they understand your requests, take a few minutes to discuss them. Providing visual aids is another useful procedure. For example, if you want chairs arranged in a unique manner, make a chart for the custodian. If you want material typed in a particular format, prepare a sample for the typist.

- In residential programs be certain that you understand the telephone and mail arrangements. Knowing where participants can obtain postage stamps, for example, seems like a trivial detail, but being able to provide this information to a nervous participant preoccupied with mailing a letter home may be a very effective means of regaining his or her attention.

- What are the room checkout procedures? What form of payment is acceptable?

There are three general guidelines that summarize our suggestions regarding physical facilities and key people.

- Remember that someone has a feeling of ownership for the facility. When in someone else's facility you are a guest. Find out who "owns" it and be sensitive to the feelings and values of that person or persons.

- View the operators of the facility as an extension of your staff. Show them the same concern, respect, and courtesy you give to your staff members.

- Be proactive. Try to anticipate requirements and problems and take action before they occur. Avoid being in a position of having to react to unanticipated events and circumstances.

ESTABLISHING CREDIBILITY

Instructor credibility, in the final analysis, is a matter of respect. For the most part, you must earn it. Participants must perceive you as competent, concerned, and confident. We have already discussed several ways to establish credibility. Arranging for appropriate introductions by other staff members can be effective. So can appropriate self-disclosure in warm-up exercises regarding experiences and accomplishments. Meals and other informal interactions provide an opportunity for participants to see another side of your personality.

Two additional means of establishing initial credibility are demonstrating enthusiasm and showing confidence in your subject and your material. Speak in positive terms, assume the audience will be interested, and whenever possible cite examples and anecdotes—war stories if you will—that give life to your subject. Practice using audiovisual materials and explaining difficult points beforehand so that you are smooth. We'll say more about presentations later, but do remember that it's difficult to grant credibility to instructors who are unenthusiastic and apologetic.

A final means of establishing credibility is, strangely enough, the effective use of mistakes. Don't make a habit of it, but when you are wrong or bungle part of a presentation, acknowledge it first, and then, if you can, turn it to your advantage. This is not always possible, but when it is, it's worth considering.

For example, an instructor in a supervision workshop had given a mid-course test to evaluate participants' performances—or such was his stated purpose to participants. His real motive was to use the test as a means of assuring that students would complete reading assignments. His experience had been that without some external pressure, many students would not keep up with the assigned readings. When they didn't, his instruction, which was based on participants' having read the materials, was difficult and less effective.

To provide reality to his test, he graded it and reported marks of excellent, good, average, and below average to the participants. They became very upset over this procedure and expressed their concerns on a mid-course evaluation and review held just after the testing incident. Resentment was high among participants. The instructor had lost credibility, and the climate was chilly.

How could he resolve the issue? Defending himself seemed fruitless, and there simply wasn't time in the short-term training program to allow for a slow return of better feelings. Consequently, he decided to turn the event into a learning situation. First, he acknowledged his underlying motive in giving the exam and explained why he had followed through with grades. Having laid himself open to a whipping at the post, he then suggested that the group approach the situation as an exercise in conflict resolution. Resolving conflicts is an important supervisory function, and, after all, this was a supervision course. His method worked very well. A few doubters remained for a while, but his openness and the competency he demonstrated for dealing with a conflict situation regained him his lost credibility.

Trainer's Tip: Credibility is earned, not advertised.

PACING

You will recall that the last step in the design phase was sequencing
the learning activities. Attention was given to both pedagogical
and climate concerns. Your schedule prescribes the pace you desire
to keep. Maintaining the pace is another matter and one that
demands your attention throughout the conducting of the program.
Here are some suggestions for maintaining the pace you desire.

☐ Preview your schedule in regard to timing just prior to beginning the program. Unanticipated circumstances, such as significant changes in predicted attendance or problems with facilities, and weather conditions may suggest altering the sequence
of events or adding activities for the specific purpose of helping
maintain the pace you desire.

☐ Humor is an effective way of maintaining a variable pace.
Humor related to the short-term training program itself is probably most effective. The subject matter, procedure, staff, and
common experiences are all fair game. Participants can often
supply useful humor if you give them the opportunity. Sometimes
you must give them permission or acknowledge by your actions
that humor is acceptable. The danger in this, of course, is that it
might encourage a wiseacre to inhibit learning by too frequent and
irrelevant humor. There are ways to deal with this, including confronting the person directly and requesting that he or she not be
disruptive.

☐ If your subject seems totally serious, then consider introducing
humor that is unrelated to it. One instructor who did short courses
on bacterial analysis of septic tank samples and similar stimulating
topics developed a collection of topical jokes, which he told with
some skill. He used these to pace his instructional programs. He
claimed that starting each session with a story helped set a favor-

able climate. He would also tell a story after particularly dry or taxing presentations. Participants learned to anticipate these, and he maintained that the stories had a reinforcing effect and thus were useful in holding the group's attention.

☐ Another factor involved in pacing a short-term training program is the concerns and values of participants for what may seem to you unimportant details. For example, if you are running behind schedule, don't cut short the coffee breaks, lunch, or informal periods. If you feel gaining time is critical, describe your concern to the participants and involve them in solving the problem.

An example of a small issue making a big difference regarding pacing is hands-on experience. In one seminar of thirty technicians, the instructor demonstrated a new electronic scope. As part of the demonstration, he invited two participants to use the instrument. For some reason, the gadget was extremely appealing, and everyone in the group wanted very much to try it. Taking time to do so would have been devastating to the pace he had set. However, he sensed that he would be viewed as arbitrary and thus resented by participants if he refused to allow them hands-on time. Being a bright and sensitive fellow, he described his dilemma to the group and volunteered to remain after the day's program and work with those who wanted to try the instrument.

☐ Finally, if you anticipate problems with pacing, talk about it with the group. If you will be moving relatively fast, for example, tell this to the group. Acknowledge that it may be frustrating or taxing and that you would prefer a slower pace but circumstances don't allow it. Then begin with the pace you had intended. Monitor the group's reaction to it, and if the frustration you anticipated develops, take a few minutes for the group to express its feelings and for you to acknowledge their validity. You may need to do this several times. It is usually unrealistic to expect a once-only reference to a difficult pace to be effective. In other words, you have to do more than say just once at the beginning, "This is going to be a tough course, gang, and we haven't much time. So we're going to move right along, and that may be frustrating." You need to continue to remind the group of that and to acknowledge several times that their frustrations are normal.

PRESENTATIONS

People vary tremendously in their ability to present or teach. All the instructional training in the world would never eliminate the gap between the brilliant presenter and the sleep peddler. Nevertheless, even though it may be impossible to learn charisma, it is possible to learn presentation ideas, which at least give you an even break as an instructor. Among those that we think are important are the following, some of which we have touched on in prior sections. See chapter 5 for a descriptive listing of instructional procedures.

Seating

The importance of seating arrangements differs with the purpose of the programs. But it is never unimportant. If writing is part of the activity, be sure adequate writing space is available for participants. (Bring extra pens or pencils and a supply of paper. Sure, it's the participants' responsibility to bring their own, but why make an issue out of a problem that you can easily solve?)

If demonstrations are included, try to arrange seating so that all participants can see. If this is impossible, and there will be movement back and forth from seats to the demonstration space, plan the movement so that it avoids confusion and waste of valuable time.

In programs that involve much discussion and interaction between participants and instructor, do everything possible to avoid seating people behind one another. Nothing inhibits discussion more than having to talk to the back of someone's head. Arrange chairs in a half circle or circle. Decide ahead of time whether you will be sitting with the group or working at a board or chart, or some of both, and arrange the chairs accordingly. Don't, for example, place yourself in a circle at the opposite end of the room from the chalkboard and then walk back and forth through the circle to the board.

When small-group discussions are used, make sure that chairs are rearranged into the original pattern *if* you want to reestablish the large group. If not, let the small-group clusters remain. Remember, finally, that while you may be moving up and down and exercising your body, the participants aren't, and chairs are hard. Give them stretch breaks if they don't occur naturally.

Neatness doesn't guarantee learning, but neither does a chaotic work space contribute to it. Clutter can contribute to confusion and direct attention away from the task of the moment.

Trainer's Tip: Get out material and equipment when you are going to use them and put them away when they have been used.

Starting and stopping

Structure sessions so that people know what to expect. Except when surprise is part of the program, tell participants what they can expect to learn and what they will be doing. One might say to a class of beginning bus drivers, "This morning we are going to study the routes in the central part of the city. You will be using the route maps in your kit and marking them with felt pens. When we finish this session, you will be able to describe about half of the routes and time schedules."

End sessions by telling participants what they have learned. For example, "This morning you learned about half of the downtown routes and demonstrated that you could describe them. Note those that may not be totally clear to you so that we can work on these routes later."

In short, begin a session by telling a group how they will be different when it is over and conclude it by pointing out how they have changed. To learn something is to make a change in oneself.

Group discussions

There are several ways to facilitate small-group discussions. There are exceptions to all these suggestions, but, in general, following them will get better results from small-group work.

Be firm about the size of the groups if you have a reason for designating a specific size. If you want to have maximum assurance that every participant talks, then obviously form groups of two and don't permit larger groups to gather. The larger the group, the easier it is for a participant to remain silent. (Silence doesn't necessarily mean nonparticipation. Some people talk less than others—thank goodness—but people who want to talk but are also shy can more easily succumb to their insecurity in larger groups.)

Be sure that the groups understand their assignments. Think about what you are going to say in making assignments. Write them out if they are more than simple. If they are complex, make copies of the assignment sheets and provide each group with one. You can check the understanding of assignments by asking someone to tell you what the participants are to do. A further way to check understanding is to visit each group briefly at the start of the small-group discussions, clarifying as the need appears.

In addition to being clear about what they are to do, also tell them the purpose of doing it. The purpose is very clear to you because you've been thinking about it. But participants haven't, and they may not perceive even the slightest connection between what they are doing and the goals of the short-term training program. You may have to state it more than once. If we see some look of confusion after being as clear as possible about the purpose of an exercise, we respond by asking, "What isn't clear?" and then attempt to clarify. While some people are willing to participate in an activity without being clear about its purpose, others aren't. Until they understand *why*, they are at best reluctant participants.

Trainer's Tip: Always give a reason for what you are doing.

It is helpful to observe groups as they work. If you plan to do this, announce that you will be moving from group to group. Avoid getting involved in the discussions except to motivate and clarify. Don't let the small groups give you a leadership role. Mostly listen and observe. What you observe can be used as examples in the follow-up total group discussions.

When there is more than one instructor, it is preferable that a group be consistently observed by the same instructor. You get to know them better and become more familiar with their concerns. If, however, the staff differs in regard to the status the participants give them or in effectiveness, the groups with the lesser status staff may feel slighted and need some kind of re-assurance.

Media

It seems superfluous to note the importance of having skill with the media you use in presentations. Nevertheless, ineptness with machines and other devices continues to destroy well-designed and well-developed presentations. Therefore, we give some simple rules.

- Never, but never, use a machine of any kind in a presentation without practicing it first.

- Always check power supplies.

- Read flip charts, slides, and chalkboards from the back of the room before using them.

- Always preview films, filmstrips, and audiovisual tapes before using.

Visual aids can help overcome the attention-span problems of overly long presentations. If used for this purpose, they should be structured so that participants perceive them as an activity, which is somewhat different from listening to your ongoing presentation. If the visuals are an integral part of your oral presentation, they are less likely to solve the attention-span problem. The choice of how you organize the visuals is often an arbitrary one. It may seem that slides, for example, should be used throughout a presentation, illustrating each point as it is made. It may be equally effective, however, to organize them as a separate follow-up presentation, thus providing a means of shifting from a straight listening activity to a watching/listening one.

All these suggestions are aimed at avoiding situations in which media misuse detracts from teaching/learning. A screen that won't stay down, a slide projector with a dirty lens, a film projector that you can't load, and a transparency with too much information get in the way of instruction. One would probably be better off without them.

Oral presentations

Probably the most frequently used "device" for presenting information in short-term training programs is the instructor. Because we rely heavily on oral presentations, it is important to do them well. If you have doubts about your own presentations, here are several ideas regarding oral presentations and interactions that we find useful.

- Speak in complete sentences. Your train of thought may be clear to you as you drop one sentence in the middle and pick up another, but it's probably confusing to your audience. They wonder what you started to say but didn't finish. Use language with which you are comfortable. Don't try to use jargon that is unfamiliar to you.

- Be sensitive to the attention span of your audience. It differs. It is a function of their background and interests, the subject matter itself, and your ability to present. In general, we try to set a thirty-minute maximum on straight information presentations. That's a long time for an audience to sit and listen unless the presenter is especially capable.

There are a number of ways to add variety to presentations. You can insert brief question-and-answer periods. This doesn't give everyone an opportunity to talk, but it is a means of varying the activity. Inserting five-to-six-minute periods for persons seated next to each other to discuss the material you have just presented does involve everyone. Combining brief work sheets with neighbors' discussions is another means. This works well when you want participants to test themselves regarding the application of a concept or skill.

Responding to questions and comments is an art in itself. It is usually helpful to repeat questions or comments before responding to them. Two purposes are served. First, you assure yourself that you understand the questions or comments and obtain clarification if need be. Second, by repeating the comment or question, you assure yourself that all participants hear it. As most of us have experienced, it is annoying to hear a speaker responding to a question that we couldn't hear.

Trainer's Tip: Don't be afraid of admitting that you don't know the answer to a question. Say you don't have the answer and, if possible, indicate you will attempt to find it.

Use questions as a means of building climate. When possible, compliment the person. "That's a good question" or "I'm glad you raised that issue" will do.

Hecklers

Occasionally one encounters stupid, rude, or hostile comments. How should these be handled? Positively—even when the participants' remarks are outrageous. Never put down participants by responding negatively to a person with an uninformed question or comment; you're risking your rapport with the group. More often than not, most of the participants identify more with one another than with you. Thus when you put one of them down for asking a "dumb question," they're likely to perceive you as being derogatory to the total group.

In the case of rude or hostile remarks, it may well be that most of the participants are on your side. But even here there is no reason for you to respond negatively. By keeping your cool you demonstrate your ability, probably maintain control of the situation, and gain respect from participants for not lowering yourself to a defensive position.

While we know of no guaranteed techniques for dealing with malcontents and hecklers, here are some general ideas to keep in mind. Separate the person's remark from the need to make the remark. Imagine that you have just completed a presentation and a participant says in a hostile tone, "I really don't think any of that is important. It isn't related to our jobs, and it's a waste of time. Why can't you get to something more practical?"

For purposes of the illustration, assume that you are very confident that your presentation is relevant, and either this fellow doesn't understand his own job or something else is bothering him. Your first reaction is probably a tightening of your stomach muscles and a desire to point out that he has failed to understand your point. The stomach reaction you'll have to live with, but you will probably be more effective by responding with something like this:

"I believe that the topic is relevant and practical. Sorry I didn't make that clear. I know it's annoying when you don't see the point of a presentation. Can you be more specific about your concern?"

With this response, you've not backed off, but you have acknowledged his concern, stated your willingness to help, and thrown the problem back at him. If he has a genuine concern about the relevancy of your presentation, he now has an opportunity to do something about it. If he doesn't, and something else is annoying him, then that will be pretty obvious.

Let's pursue this example further. Imagine that the participant's real gripe is not with your presentation at all but with his being forced to attend the short-term training program. He didn't want to come and is mad at his supervisor who put pressure on him to attend—and probably angry with himself for not standing up to his supervisor. He doesn't accept your offer of clarification, nor does he back off.

"Well, we disagree about that," he says. "The problem with all these training sessions is that you guys haven't any on-the-job experience. You don't know what it's like out there in the real world. It's all theory."

What to do? The situation can deteriorate into a ridiculous argument unless you take some action. This fellow seems bound to pursue his discontent. One way to take the wind out of his sails is to grant him time, but at your convenience. You could say, "You seem concerned; I'm certainly willing to talk with you. Let's meet before lunch, and maybe you can resolve your frustration. But this isn't an appropriate time, and I would like to go on with our program."

The general principle with situations like this is to acknowledge the person's feelings and make it clear that there is a problem—it is not yours, but make some offer to assist.

Late arrivers

What about late arrivers? Do you postpone beginning until they come? Whenever possible, don't. It is disrespectful of the participants who arrived on time. It is also a message to the group that the schedule is not important and that tardiness will be tolerated.

As noted earlier, opening sessions may be the biggest exception to this suggestion. People may have trouble finding the facility or getting a parking space or run into other difficulties. Opening instructions may be so essential that you can't begin until all are present.

That is the time to make your intentions known. Be as clear as possible.

"I like to begin on time, so please be ready to start at the times indicated. We won't wait for latecomers."

Then do as you say.

STAFF-PARTICIPANT RELATIONSHIPS

The crucial decision has to be made by the staff—what kind of relationship you want with participants. How formal do you wish to be? Having made that decision, it is then a question of selecting appropriate behaviors—manner of address, where you sit at mealtimes, dress, and manner and jargon to be used.

Seducing the instructor

There are many ways of being seduced by participants apart from the obvious one. Some will demand private time and attention. If you give too much to a few, this can reverberate on the climate as a whole. Here is our rogue's gallery of seducers.

Teacher's pet   Small gifts—even apples! Sometimes newspaper clippings pertaining to what you have been teaching. Be careful; this might simply register keenness.

Cotrainer   The one who always engages you in eye contact, especially when supposedly talking to someone else. What is really being communicated is: "You and I really know all about this, don't we? How can we make it simple enough for the others to understand?"

Prosecuting counsel   Attacks every point you make. The seduction here is to play the game of defending. Then you're hooked.

Sex symbol   Applies to both sexes. They gaze at you with meaningful expressions and winsome smiles. They always stand too close and manage to touch you at every opportunity. Delightful, but deadly—for the climate, that is.

Bosom pal   The overfriendly one who invites you home, brings the family for you to meet, slaps you on the back, and asks searching personal questions.

Disciple   Praises you at each opportunity. Can't wait to spread the word.

Neurotic   The one who sits staring into space, looking nervous, totally uninvolved. May keep jotting down notes that obviously have nothing to do with the course. Turns up late—or not at all. Watch this one. May be genuinely uninterested, in which case you need to find out why. May also be genuinely upset and carrying a lot of baggage.

Saboteur   Unlike the prosecuting counsel, this one doesn't nitpick. This one makes sweeping attempts to sabotage the whole procedure. Interrupts constantly, makes loud asides, turns up late, or leaves early. It's important to check this one out at first coffee break; otherwise a great deal of your time and energy can be taken up. People who try to sabotage usually have a reason for doing it.

Sneak   Comes to tell you about the nasty things that people are saying about you—usually naming them.

Troublemaker   The one who takes you aside and tells you confidentially about having problems with one of the other staff members. There's only one solution—tell the person to sort it out directly with the staff member involved. Don't be seduced into being message carrier or negotiator.

Trainer's Tip: Know the ways by which you can be seduced by participants.

You are the key

You are the most important determinant of group climate. What can you do to foster a healthy climate?

- Learn participants' names quickly and use them; memorize their name tags. Play the names game. Everyone sits in a circle. You begin by saying, "I'm Barrie." The next person says, "I'm Sue; this is Barrie." The next continues, "I'm Jack; this is Sue and Barrie," and so on. We have used this with groups of up to forty participants. It is well worth the ten to fifteen minutes involved. By the end of it, most people know one another's names; it also serves as an excellent icebreaker.

- Talk to participants outside the sessions. Don't form a staff clique.

- Hold staff sessions unobtrusively. Staff members should distribute themselves around at mealtime. Don't all sit together.

- Participate in some exercises.

- Buy a round of drinks.

- Join in some social events.

- In a serial course, make a note to ask people about things that you talked about in a previous session. "How did that project work out?" "Is your son any better now?"

- Don't get drunk.

- Don't talk to only the attractive or handsome members of a course.

- Try to deal with any special requests.

- Don't use sexist jokes or put down ethnic groups.

- And, needless to say, no sex with participants! Much has been written and discussed about this topic. Some trainers claim that courses are no different from other spheres of life and there should be no special rules. We do not agree. There are differences. The trainer is in a powerful position. A residential course, in particular, is like the birth of a new culture, and the staff members are in very privileged positions. Their very power will make them attractive to some participants. To use that power sexually seems to us to be a form of exploitation.

It is not the only form of exploitation that trainers are guilty of. Some play out guru trips, others their needs to be loved and admired, some their need to exercise control and manipulate people. Where we have encountered this, the effect on group climate has usually been disastrous. Some participants are morally outraged, others feel jealous, most will be distracted—watching the two people involved, speculating, talking about them. In other words, not doing what they are there to do—learn.

STAFF RELATIONSHIPS

We would like to present a number of questions for staff to follow as a guide. This list will obviously reflect our personalities. You can add your own. Remember, the way the staff members behave toward one another will determine to a large extent how participants will behave with one another. You are important role models. Be aware of what you are modeling.

Check out with one another about operating styles. Before you begin a course, you should be able to list the strengths and weaknesses of each staff member's style, including your own.

We have developed interview questions for quickly finding out as much as possible about a new staff member. It is suggested that, where appropriate, two of you interview each other. It probably will not take more than thirty minutes altogether.

Interview Questions for Getting to Know Your Colleague

1. What are your strengths as a trainer?
2. What are your weaknesses?
3. Describe a successful training experience you have had.
4. Describe an unsuccessful training experience.
5. What do you find most difficult to live with in colleagues?
6. What types of trainers cause you the most problems?
7. How much say do you think participants should have in running a course?

8. Have you done courses similar to the one we are planning for now? Describe them.
9. Do you have any technical expertise with equipment?
10. How do you relax in or away from a course?

Ensure that one staff member has overall charge of the program and that someone is responsible for each session. Even if it's a joint session, someone has to start and end it, taking responsibility for the timing. It won't happen by chance. Any good tennis doubles team has it all worked out in advance. If you leave it to chance, the ball goes down the middle, with each player leaving it to the other.

Don't be a clique. For example, humor is a tremendous aid to climate building but not when it is excluding—when staff members use in-jokes and have a great time but the participants are in the dark.

Sometimes it pays to work out staff differences in front of the group. This can be effective modeling behavior if you are confident about your relationship. At other times it might be inappropriate. The group may feel that you should not be taking up their time with this.

On the basis of known strengths, work out in advance who is responsible for doing what. Some people are better at task functions—initiating, giving or seeking information or opinions, elaborating, coordinating, evaluating, energizing, recording; other trainers are better at maintenance functions—encouraging, harmonizing, compromising, keeping everyone involved, making sure everyone feels valued, watching the group process. Rarely do strength splits follow so neatly. In addition, some staff members are better at socializing, making jokes, partying, staying up late, and so on. See how you can complement one another.

If two or more staff members are running a session, it is often a good idea for them not to bunch up front. If they are distributed around the group, there is less chance of their missing anything important, and they will also appear less formidable.

Don't ignore status differences. If you have a star on your team, recognize this. For example, in small-group work, each group will want to spend some time with the star.

Have ongoing review sessions whenever necessary—usually at the end of a day. We often call a review session after lunch. We eat with the participants, then explain that we need to have some time to review proceedings, and meet over coffee. We sometimes use the design whereby any staff member can call a review session at such a time, but we do not have one automatically.

MONITORING AND RENEGOTIATING

In the next chapter, we describe several ways to evaluate short-term training programs when they have been completed. However, one kind of evaluation is aimed at discovering flaws or problems during the actual workshop so that they can be corrected. This kind of evaluation depends upon an ongoing monitoring of the short-term training program. If you want to be on top of what is taking place, monitoring is essential. It is important to know about both the learning that is occurring and the state of the climate.

A discussion of monitoring methods will be taken up in chapter 8. Here we want to know what kinds of problems can occur and what can be done about them. We have alluded to some of the possible problems before. They include schedule breakdown, lack of interest, inaccurate estimates of participants' abilities, new needs, personality conflicts, illness, and problems with facilities. In some cases the solution is essentially up to the staff. Change the pace, clarify presentations, provide more individual attention to some participants, have the equipment repaired, or speak with the cook about the meal schedule.

There are other times, however, when solutions may appropriately involve the participants as well as the staff. The most effective approach, in other words, may be to renegotiate the contract.

This points up the importance of having a clear understanding of the initial contract between staff and participants and of the assumptions that underlie it. It is difficult to renegotiate what was poorly understood in the first place.

There are several ways to renegotiate a contract, and they all involve discussions. The first task is usually to clarify the issues involved. When agreement has been reached regarding these, alternative solutions can be identified. Small group discussions, brainstorming, and listing priorities are ways of identifying alternative solutions. The group then must decide which alternative they will use. This can be done by taking a majority rule vote or by reaching a consensus. The latter denotes general agreement, but some would personally not choose the alternative selected.

An example may be helpful. We ran a two-day short-term training program aimed at teaching volunteers in a gerontology program how to identify and use community resource agencies. We assumed that the participants had fairly sophisticated helping skills and experience working with an older population. By mid-morning of the first day, however, it was clear that at least half of the participants were new to volunteer work. Their helping skills were minimal, and they had no experience with the problems of older people. All agreed that the original contract—identifying and learning to use community agencies in helping older people—was unrealistic for half of the participants and that it should be reexamined and possibly renegotiated.

What was the problem? All agreed that it was that half the group didn't meet the prerequisite of the short-term training program and thus would not benefit from the program as planned. In small group discussions, they identified the following alternative solutions:

1. Cancel the program.
2. Cancel the program for those who didn't have the prerequisite.
3. Redesign the program and focus on teaching helping skills.
4. Split the group into two, with one group following the original plan and the other studying helping skills.
5. Have the experienced participants help the nonexperienced learn helping skills.

All alternatives were a compromise, but consensus was reached regarding the last alternative. No alternative was preferred by all.

It is important to see that in addition to renegotiating the contract, staff and participants were aware of and accepted the implications. They knew that they would not be doing exactly what they had expected but agreed that the changed program was better than the other alternatives.

In extreme cases, contract renegotiation can also involve the contractor. This would be important if it became clear that for reasons beyond their control, the trainers could not produce the learning called for in the contract. Because contracts between trainers and contractor have the advantage of being made before a short-term training program begins, it should be possible to avoid serious unrealistic expectations resulting from confusion regarding such variables as time, facilities, and participant minimum prerequisites.

WHOLESALE CHANGES

The issue of changing short-term training programs while they are in progress has emerged several times in our discussion. Each time that it has, we have seen changes as responses to unanticipated problems or circumstances.

In addition, instructors make changes as a result of some insight or bright new idea. You may have discovered the perfect answer to your training problem at the eleventh hour. But the odds are usually pretty good that if you allowed your brilliant new idea to stand the test of a few hours time, its glow might diminish and possible flaws appear.

It has been our experience that usually the last-minute revolutionary ideas aren't so unpredictable as one might think. They can be a reaction to a short-term training program design with which you are basically dissatisfied. Thus, it is usually worthwhile to ask yourself throughout the development phase whether you are actually satisfied with the program design. If you have doubts, reexamining the design at that point may be very productive—and a better plan than counting on last-minute inspiration to give you a more satisfactory program.

Trainer's Tip: While inspiration can strike all of us, be cautious about making wholesale changes in programs.

ONGOING PUBLIC RELATIONS

The conducting phase has more direct impact on the relationships you develop with your various publics than any of the other phases of the short-term training programs. What you do in conducting the program is what participants experience. The reports they make are all that other people know about your programs. Your future work, whether it be within your organization or for other clients, will be influenced by the reputation you build with the completion of each additional training program.

Program quality is extremely important in building a favorable reputation, but sometimes that alone is insufficient. Other efforts are needed regarding issues not directly related to program quality.

We need to be aware that offhand remarks, jokes, or humorously intended comments concerning the organization or its personnel can be misinterpreted, misquoted, and the source of rumors and misunderstandings. In a program for schoolteachers, for example, we were attempting to establish some rapport with the group, identifying with them as instructors. We made the humorously intended comment that we had been administrators for a time, until we realized that if one had any talent at all, administration was a waste of time. Following the program, we had an evaluation meeting with the superintendent of the contracting school district.

His opening remark was said very seriously. "I understand you knocked administrators every chance you got." It took twenty minutes to clarify the issue and clear the air—and we suspect that some of the relationship damage was never repaired.

We're not suggesting that all possible sources of conflict be avoided—that would be impossible because one person's oblivion is another's chief concern.

A related issue is the threat your program is to others in the organization, especially administrators. Many training programs are designed to bring about changes. Changes in procedures, methods, values, and attitudes. Change is often threatening, especially to those who are not in on it and to those who are comfortable with the existing procedures and values.

Your program may have, unbeknown to you, significant political implications. There may be resentment against those selected to participate or implications for promotions and other personnel changes. It may have all kinds of symbolic and real meaning within the contracting organization.

There is probably little that you can do to avoid issues of this kind, but you can work toward keeping them from damaging your public relations. Here are a few suggested dos and don'ts.

- Be a neutral observer of nonprogram issues that arise. Acknowledge their existence but don't take sides.

- Most organizations have one or more hierarchies, and it is helpful to understand those that affect your program.

- Other hierarchy problems involve differences between real and nominal power. An understanding of who actually makes decisions and who makes things move provides guidelines for public relations.

- Discover the norms of the organization. What are the limits of acceptability? We arrived in open-necked shirts to contract for a seminar at a client's facility. It was midsummer, and the temperature was more than 100 degrees Fahrenheit and the humidity 85 percent. When we entered the large company dining area for lunch, we noticed that every man in the room was dressed in a shirt and tie. We asked our host whether this reflected a company policy, since it seemed that, given the temperature, a few people at least would have chosen more comfortable clothes. "You should have been here before," responded our host. "Only since the first of the year have colored shirts been permissible." All we're suggesting is that you learn the local norms. Knowledge can help you avoid pointless hassles and misunderstandings.

Trainer's Tip: Discover the formal and informal norms of the organization before beginning the program.

- Keep the training program paramount in your own mind. It should be the only topic on your agenda. One of the best ways to promote a professional image and strong public relations is to demonstrate that the program is the only reason you are there. It occupies all your efforts and concerns. Demonstrate that you have neither the interest nor time to become entangled in other issues.

- Don't bad-mouth organizations or people. It may sometimes be a tempting means of establishing rapport and identifying something in common with participants, but it has a way of working against you. There is usually no function served by bad-mouthing except temporary identification or a cheap laugh.

- Don't reinforce unrealistic expectations. You have a fairly accurate idea of what participants will gain from your program, but they may confuse hopes with reality. It is better for public relations to get them to readjust their aspirations than to leave the program having experienced a large disappointment.

TERMINATION

There are three groups from whom you will eventually have to take your leave: the participants, colleagues, and the contracting organization.

Just as you need to spend time planning for everyone's entry to the course, so also do you need to anticipate the end of the course.

Participants

Many people have difficulty saying good-bye to people they may not see again or even closing an experience with people they will see again. Parallels with death and dying have been made by some writers on group behavior, and there is no doubt that after an intensive residential course, for example, some participants do undergo a mourning experience. This, of course, is at one extreme only. But even at the other extreme, a presession course still has a termination issue.

How can you help people leave and, indeed, take your leave of participants?

We always have some evaluation, even if it is only a half-day course (see chapter 8). This gives participants an opportunity to give positive and negative feedback. We usually ask for the negative first. "In what ways could the course have been improved?" This means that you can end with the positive, which helps send everyone away on an "upper." We always like to give feedback to them. Usually this will only be very general, but we always try to find something positive to say about the course and about the participants in particular.

There are often "reentry" problems for people who have been in a block or residential course. Try to give people an opportunity to work through these. We use some type of applications-to-work exercise in which participants have to summarize their learning and apply it to their back-home situation—whatever that is.

Frequently we use a fantasy exercise. Get people to close their eyes and imagine they are on a magic carpet. It is taking them back from the course to their work or home. The leader then asks them a series of questions, and they try silently to visualize what is happening to them. The questions vary with the course. For example, Where are you going? What will you be leaving behind? How do you feel about that? What do you feel as you approach your destination? Whom do you see first? What do you say and do? What have they been doing while you have been away? (Especially important if the participant has been on a psychologically uplifting week's course while the spouse has been coping alone with three children!) It is three days later, what are you feeling now? It is three months later, what are you feeling now? Then you bring people back to the present, and they discuss their experiences in pairs, trios, or total group.

We often try to end a course with what Sir Thomas Beecham called a lollipop—a goody for a good audience. An example is what we call a positive strokes exercise. The terminology comes from transactional analysis and refers to any positive act of recognition from one person to another. After the concept has been explained, people are told that they will all have a half sheet of flip-chart paper taped to their backs. Armed with magic markers, for fifteen minutes or so they have to write on fellow participants' papers as many positive thoughts or feelings they have about them as they can. The experience is usually hilariously chaotic. At the end of the exercise, the participants look at their own stroke sheets and perhaps even read out loud the three they like most.

Another idea is to ask participants to write letters to one another expressing positive thoughts.

End up with a party, or sometimes even a glass of sherry or wine paid for by the staff will do.

You can kill off the group ritually. The group hold hands while you give a eulogy for the course. They then walk backward until only their fingertips are touching. You ask them to take one more step backward, clap your hands, and announce that the group togetherness is over.

Beware of reunionitis! Some participants find it difficult to let go of the experience. Don't get caught up in their plans for reunions. They probably won't materialize, you will probably not be free, and you won't be paid either!

Colleagues

It is good for staff to end on an upper, too. Share any positive feelings with colleagues. Sometimes it might be appropriate to do this publicly.

An immediate debriefing session is valuable if you all have the time and energy. If you don't do this immediately, it often does not get done at all because of different work schedules. This kind of session is of special value, too, after a bad training experience. You will have an opportunity to discharge feelings and support one another before going home and dumping the bad feelings on someone else.

Take your leave of all the people who helped you run the course—janitors, secretaries, hotel managers, cooks, and anyone else involved. It's polite, they deserve it if they really have helped, and you may be training there again.

Pack up your equipment. Go through your checklist in reverse. Plan your own reentry!

Organization

Sometimes the termination takes place at the end of the course, and you take your leave from your contractor. Often you will be reporting back to the organization later. In addition to any verbal feedback, ensure that you provide a written report that gives your evaluation on whether the original goals and outcomes have been achieved. An in-house trainer can always send a written memo to the boss describing how the program fared.

Trainer's Tip: *After a course, always make personal contact with your contractor.*

If appropriate, send your invoice for fee and expenses with your written report.

8 Evaluation

KINDS OF EVALUATION

The final phase of the short-term training model is concerned with answering the basic question, Did you accomplish your goals? Obviously, it is not that simple. In the first place, your program probably had several goals. In the second, the answers are probably not yes or no but partially. There are also questions regarding costs, public relations, and future program changes. While program evaluation may seem to be a simple task at first glance, it can evolve into a complex effort.

How much? How good?

Evaluation actually involves asking two kinds of questions. One is How much? and the other is How good?

The first question—How much?—is concerned with measurement. The answer by itself has no meaning in relation to how good your program has been. The answer tells you only how much your program accomplished. Deciding upon the worth of that accomplishment is not a matter of measurement. It is a value judgment.

Imagine that out of twenty participants in your course, fifteen scored fifty on the final examination. Is that good? There's no way to decide, is there? If we add the fact that the highest possible score was 100, can you judge whether those who scored fifty were good? Not yet. What if you also know that the remaining five students all scored above ninety-five? Now is a score of fifty good? We still can't say. All we can say is that 25 percent of the group made scores higher than fifty.

Let's further imagine that in the group of twenty, there are ten participants who are new to the subject and ten who are very experienced. You expected the experienced people to make nearly perfect scores and the students new to the field to score no better than fifty. Now, with these values in mind, you can judge the performance, at least in a gross manner. All the new participants scored fifty, and thus their performance was good. Five of the experienced students performed at expectation (nearly perfect), which is good. However, the remaining five experienced students did not perform up to expectation, so their scores would not be judged good.

Thus we can answer the How good? question only in regard to some value. How good in regard to X? You or someone else must define X.

We always assume that information is collected and used as a basis for evaluation. Sometimes, in actuality, it is not. We'll discuss that problem below. But in the remainder of this discussion, evaluation means feedback/evaluation.

Evaluation criteria

There are three types of criteria or standards that can be used for evaluating short-term training programs: (1) immediate criteria, (2) process criteria, and (3) outcome criteria.

Immediate criteria refer to preprogram reviews of staff and facilities. Some people would question our calling this evaluation. We believe it is—in the sense of measuring the extent to which you are prepared to conduct your program and then deciding whether you are satisfied. The procedure is similar to the checklists that airline pilots use prior to takeoff. They evaluate the aircraft's readiness for flight. You can evaluate your short-term training program's readiness for conducting.

Process criteria refer to participants' reactions to teaching procedures and learning climate. Having procedures operate as planned and maintaining a supportive climate don't guarantee that participants will learn, but they do set the stage for learning. Thus it pays to monitor the process to assure that the program is operating as planned and that participants view it favorably. In large part, using process criteria consists of obtaining participants' reactions to the experience you are providing.

Neither immediate nor process criteria reveal how much students learn. To find that out, we must turn to outcome criteria. At this point the problem of evaluation can become complex, depending upon the nature of the outcomes and the kind of measures you want. For example, consider a short-term training program for service technicians. The goal is to teach them how to service and repair a new model of a photocopy machine. One outcome measure would be a paper and pencil test at the end of the program. In order to be comfortable with this outcome, you would need to assume that there is a high correlation between test scores and level of on-the-job performance. Let's say that you aren't willing to assume that. Then you might want to use a hands-on demonstration at the completion of the program as an outcome measure. If you wanted to be absolutely sure of your outcome, you would need to observe participants on the job and determine their level of performance under real conditions.

Compare that situation with a supervisors' human relations short-term training program. Imagine that one of the goals is to learn how to deal effectively with conflict. That, in turn, involves people learning to be more open about their values and aspirations. Now, how do you measure whether a participant is more open about values and desires at the end of the program? Essentially, you have to believe participants' self-reports. If they say they are more open, then they are. You could devise simulations of conflict situations and observe their behaviors and perhaps disagree with their self-reports—but why is your observation any better than theirs?

Even more difficult, in regard to outcome measures, are programs that have changes in attitudes as goals. Except for sophisticated psychological tests, you have little choice other than to believe participants when they report a change in attitude. Most measures, such as questionnaires and simulations, are highly susceptible to faking.

There are many nontechnical subjects, however, for which outcome measures can be developed. The important consideration is identifying specific behaviors that are acceptable instances of the outcomes. For example, consider a short-term training program in child rearing. One goal is to have more pleasant relationships between parents and their children. That's a bit vague, but if we are willing to use "reduction in number of unpleasant encounters per day" as an indication of more pleasant relationships, then we have a useful outcome measure.

Why evaluate?

Why be concerned about evaluating short-term training programs? In the case of technical programs, the answer seems obvious. Contractors pay for people to learn to do something. In addition to wanting to know whether they got their money's worth, it is often important to assess participants' learning before assigning them new responsibilities. It is a good idea, to say the least, to know the results of a short-term training program on marksmanship before participants take up their duties as security guards. The more specifically the short-term training program is related to desired behaviors, the more critical is program evaluation. While it would be nice if participants in a couples' group were more pleasant to one another, it would only be disappointing if they discovered that they hadn't learned the necessary relationship skills. In contrast, at the end of the lifesaving course for swimming-pool guards, it is essential that we know whether or not participants can perform mouth-to-mouth resuscitation.

As trainers, most of us have a commitment to ourselves to improve our work. Evaluating current efforts can be an excellent source of information for improving those efforts.

Finally, evaluation activities can contribute to climate. They tell participants that we are concerned with them and their learning. When we ask for participant reactions, we are opening ourselves to criticism, and most participants realize that and probably respect us for it.

Let us again emphasize the importance of clear goals. The most careful and systematic evaluation won't tell us very much if program goals are unclear. If you aren't clear about what you want to achieve, then it's impossible to know whether you've achieved it. It's that simple, and it's not a matter of measurement. Thus, the clearer one specifies program goals during the design phase, the more likely effective feedback and evaluation can be accomplished.

IMMEDIATE CRITERIA

Immediate criteria involve the use of "have you got" and "have you done" checklists prior to beginning programs. The checklists in several of the previous chapters can be used for this purpose. They cover the following:

Staff assignments
  Instructor
  Administration
  Personnel

Media
  Hardware availability
  Hardware operability
  Software availability

Participant concerns
  Room
  Meals
  Transportation
  Emergencies

Facilities
  Utilities
  Furniture
  Clerical support

The list is intended to be very inclusive and is thus overly complex for many short-term training programs. Modify it, or design one that better meets the needs of your situation.

The reason for our urging you to use a formal preprogram

evaluation using immediate criteria is the tremendous potential importance of small concerns to the success of a short-term training program. Forgotten electrical extension cords and burned-out projector lights have caused problems out of proportion to their seeming importance.

PROCESS FEEDBACK AND EVALUATION

In most short-term training programs, participants have something to say about the goals. Even in highly structured technical programs, participants usually have some influence regarding what they personally want emphasized in the instructional program. In addition, they may have other goals, such as widening professional acquaintances and exploring job opportunities. In less structured programs, participants may have a great deal of latitude regarding their goals. In some programs, personal goal setting is the first task they face.

Goal clarification

Whatever the structure of a short-term training program, it is beneficial for participants to spend time clarifying their goals. Clear goals are the foundation of effective learning. They also make it possible for participants and staff to compare program purposes with individual expectations.

One way of doing initial goal clarification is to form pairs of participants at the very beginning of the workshop. Self-selected partners are preferable, and in order to make considered selections, participants need information. One approach is to use the warm-up exercises described in chapter 7. In smaller groups simply having each person introduce himself or herself, together with a brief biography, may work.

Another method is to use triads, thus reducing the possibility of a very poor match of persons. When you have formed pairs or triads, distribute the Goal Clarification Form and ask each participant to follow the instructions.

GOAL CLARIFICATION FORM

Instructions: Take five minutes to think through and answer questions 1 and 2. Be as clear as you can.

1. What do you most want to learn from this experience? List several goals you may have in mind.
2. What assumptions are you making about the program? What are your expectations that you have developed?

Discussion for question 1: Read your answers to each other and exchange ideas and discuss in the light of the following questions:

1. Is the goal specific enough to permit direct planning and action?
2. Does the goal require personal action or effort on your part— does it involve you personally?
3. Is the goal realistic? Can significant progress be made in the time available in the workshop?
4. How can others in the workshop help you work on these goals?

Discussion for question 2: Read aloud your answers to question 2 and discuss with these questions:

1. Are your assumptions and expectations consistent with what the instructor has said?
2. Are there things you want to find out and clarify?

At this point, each of you may feel the need to revise your goal descriptions, and you may rewrite them to your satisfaction. Keep them for later reference.

What you do with feedback partners depends on the length of your program. When programs are a half day or less, we suggest providing a few minutes at the end for partners to review goals and estimate progress. Suggest that they discuss the following questions:

What part of my goal(s) did I achieve?
How do I know? Give examples of achievement.
What are the most useful outcomes for me?
What would I do differently in another similar program?

In longer programs, you may want partners to meet briefly and discuss these and similar questions at the end of each half day. In that case, many participants find that keeping a diary of their thoughts, ideas, and important experiences helps them gain more from the program. The final meeting of partners can be somewhat longer, providing an opportunity to do a final review and assessment. An extension of this activity, which provides feedback to the staff and also lets participants compare their self-evaluation with that of others besides partners, is to spend time in the total group having people give short statements recognizing the achievements and disappointments during the program.

Session feedback

Another effective means of obtaining ongoing feedback is to use the Session Feedback form that follows. It is useful in almost any short-term training program. We recommend using it with each session or period that stands alone and lasts for an hour or longer.

Items 1 and 2 provide quick indications of the students' interest in the session and their perception of its relevance.

Item 3 obtains their reactions to the teaching/learning procedures used in the session. You need to list the three learning methods used in the session that you want rated.

Item 4 gives you a quick check on the extent to which you made your main point, and item 5 invites open-ended suggestions.

Participants can complete the form in less than a minute. You can scan the responses quickly and obtain a general impression of the students' feedback. If it is negative, you may want to hold a brief discussion to clarify their reactions.

SESSION FEEDBACK

Session:
Date:
Time:

By providing the information requested below, you will help us strengthen future sessions. Thank you.

1. In general, I thought today's session was

Very Dull	Mostly Dull	So-So	Mostly Interesting	Very Interesting
1	2	3	4	5

2. In regard to its usefulness, now or in the future, the substance of today's session was

No Use	Little Use	Some Use	Considerable Use	Highly Useful
1	2	3	4	5

3. Please rate the learning methods used in today's session.

Poor	Fair	Average	Good	Excellent
1	2	3	4	5

1. _____
2. _____
3. _____

4. In your opinion, what was the major concept or topic with which this session was concerned?

5. Any suggestions or comments?

Climate feedback

In residential programs it is also important to monitor noninstructional aspects of the program. Participants' reactions to unsatisfactory living conditions, for example, can affect the learning climate.

One method for monitoring this, as well as instructional concerns, is the Problem/Solutions Box. Place a small box where it is easily accessible. Tell participants they are invited to note complaints about anything pertaining to the program on three-by-five-inch cards and drop them into the box. The only condition is that on the other side of the card they include at least one suggestion for solving the problem. Check the box every half day and share the problems with the group. To have the group deal with problems its members identify can also help build solidarity and contribute to climate.

Another related procedure for obtaining feedback is to post a Rumors List. Such a sheet has two columns, providing space for the rumor and the comments.

Post the sheet at an appropriate place and state the following rules: "Anyone wanting a rumor clarified may write it in the left column. Anyone having facts or valid information related to the rumor is invited to respond in the right column. Both staff and participants may use these columns."

RUMORS LIST

BEING SAID: THE TRUTH:

_____   _____

_____   _____

_____   _____

_____   _____

_____   _____

_____   _____

_____   _____

The Rumors List is most applicable in programs that extend over a period of several weeks. During this length of time, groups can take on characteristics of a small community. As the group interaction becomes more complex, it gets to know itself. While the forming of a community spirit or sense can facilitate learning, it can also lead to problems. Idiosyncrasies of people emerge, conflicts of various kinds develop, and competition for leadership roles may come about. Some participants may feel socially isolated or rejected, and others may experience feelings of frustration and failure. Such conditions nurture rumors. Thus it is important to maintain channels of communication that are open and easily accessible.

Another systematic method of obtaining feedback is simply to schedule time for the group to discuss the progress of the program and air any concerns. Such meetings can be brief. They need not deteriorate into gripe sessions if the ground rules are clear. For example, fifteen minutes at the close of each day might be set aside as a feedback session. The agenda might be as follows:

• Report on actions taken in response to previous feedback sessions.

• Handle problems or concern—state, clarify, and assign responsibility for follow-up, if appropriate.

• List positive observations about the day.

Ending on a positive note may appear a little contrived, but scheduling positive strokes can be effective. People have a tendency to talk about their problems and negative experiences and not mention the pleasant things that happen to them. You can structure feedback sessions that emphasize looking at positive experiences as well as identifying problems.

Whatever methods you use, ongoing process evaluation can make tremendous contributions to the success of short-term training programs.

End-of-course feedback

There are several ways to obtain feedback regarding the total training program from the perspective of process. One is an open-ended discussion. Another is an open-ended written response.

More structured evaluations of process can be obtained through forms, thereby assuring that you will obtain responses to the same issues from all participants. Two types of forms are illustrated.

The first, for a course designed to teach basic human relations helping skills, asks participants to rate each of the major course activities according to a four-point scale. An additional option is to have participants distribute 200 merit points among the major activities. When using this procedure, be sure that participants can recognize the activities by the titles you list on your evaluation form.

The second form illustrates a combination of structured and open-ended evaluation. The illustration is taken from a workshop on mid-career change in which we were interested in reactions to procedures and descriptions of changes in relevant behavior. The twelve questions on the form try to get at outcomes measures via participant descriptions. Obviously, there is no practical way to check the validity of their reports. That's simply a limitation we shall have to live with.

COURSE EVALUATION

Instructions: Please rate each instructional activity in the first column according to the following scale: 1 = very effective, 2 = of some value, 3 = little or no value, 4 = detracted from course.

Then, in the second column, distribute 200 merit points among the activities.

	Rating	Merit
1. Definition of helping presentation.	_____	_____
2. Self-assessment as a helper exercise.	_____	_____
3. Defining objectives exercise.	_____	_____
4. Communications skills exercise.	_____	_____
5. Systems analysis approach presentation.	_____	_____
6. Goal-gaining tools exercise.	_____	_____
7. Reinforcement exercise.	_____	_____
8. Decision-making exercise.	_____	_____
9. Behavior observation exercise.	_____	_____
10. Behavior description exercise.	_____	_____
11. Strategies model presentation.	_____	_____
12. In service to their country exercise.	_____	_____
13. Diane Deaumont exercise.	_____	_____
14. Bernie Long (case study).	_____	_____
15. Ms. Millie Murphy.	_____	_____
16. Miscellaneous comments.	_____	_____
17. Helping . . . the text.	_____	_____
18. Research cards.	_____	_____
19. Strategy reports.	_____	_____
20. _____	_____	_____

CHANGING CAREERS WORKSHOP EVALUATION

Please respond to items 1 through 13 as indicated. Thank you.

1. Following is a list of major activities in which you participated during the workshop. Please indicate your evaluation of each activity by checking a point on the scales provided.

	USELESS	SOME VALUE	MORE USEFUL THAN NOT	VERY USEFUL	EXCELLENT
a. Doing my thing	—	—	—	—	—
b. Critical life event grid	—	—	—	—	—
c. Knowing yourself	—	—	—	—	—
d. Constraints (Sues)	—	—	—	—	—
e. Constraints and Decisions	—	—	—	—	—
f. Job satisfaction/ Dissatisfaction	—	—	—	—	—
g. Major life decisions	—	—	—	—	—
h. Stress presentation and scale	—	—	—	—	—
i. Leisure activities	—	—	—	—	—
j. Decision-making exercise	—	—	—	—	—
k. Game plan	—	—	—	—	—
l. Back home	—	—	—	—	—
m. The workbook	—	—	—	—	—
n. _____	—	—	—	—	—

2. What understandings or insights do you have concerning yourself that you didn't have before the workshop? Give both general and specific.

3. What useful skills and/or information regarding career planning have you acquired?

4. Using what you learned in the workshop, how will you find information concerning activities relating to the following:

    Job
    Vocation
    Leisure

5. What benefits did you receive from the decision-making procedure covered in the workshop?

6. Look over the workshop goals you wrote in your log for Monday, Tuesday, and Wednesday. Write the goals here.

    Monday:
    Tuesday:
    Wednesday:

7. What workshop activities served to accomplish the goals you wrote for each day?

    Monday's goals:
    Tuesday's goals:
    Wednesday's goals:

8. What was not covered in the workshop that you would have liked to have included?

9. What decision, if any, concerning your life have you made as a result of this workshop?

10. What do you plan to do to implement that decision?

11. How did you learn about the workshop?

12. Would you recommend it to a friend wanting to make a career change?

13. Would you have attended the workshop had it not been sponsored by the university?

Self-monitoring

You can also be a source of useful feedback. Simply reflect on events as they occur, or structure your observations more formally. If you want to do the latter, the following form may be useful.

INSTRUCTOR'S SELF-MONITORING FORM

Instructions: After each session, or each hour or so during the program, ask yourself the following questions:

1. How clear is the group regarding the purpose of the current activity?

All Seem Clear	Most Seem Clear	Half and Half	Most Seem Confused

2. Upon what am I basing this conclusion?

Their statements _____
My observations _____
My hunch _____
Don't know _____

3. How is the learning climate?

Very Supportive	OK	Problems for Some	Debilitating

4. What action would be helpful at this time?

OUTCOMES EVALUATION

We will not attempt to present any more than a few ideas regarding outcomes evaluations. The subject is relatively complex and requires a technical understanding of various measurement and statistical concepts and procedures. The reader interested in learning about outcomes evaluations is urged to read appropriate references listed in chapter 9. The following comments can serve as an introduction to some of the main concerns and issues regarding outcomes evaluation.

There is some confusion about evaluating short-term training programs in regard to outcomes. Within the field of education, outcomes refer to changes in the behavior or attitudes of participants. When short-term training programs involve learning concepts, information, and skills, outcomes evaluation is a matter of measuring how much participants learned and deciding whether that amount is sufficient.

An increasing number of short-term training programs are concerned with goals that appear to be difficult to define in terms of concepts, information, and skills. Programs, for example, that have such goals as "realizing your human potential," "getting to know yourself," "expanding your awareness," and "raising your consciousness" often do not translate those abstract goal statements into behaviors that can be observed and measured. Yet many people who produce short-term training programs of this nature are interested in doing outcomes evaluation. The problem, of course, is one of trying to measure outcomes that have never been stated in measurable terms.

The solution that some trainers have chosen is to substitute process variables for outcomes behaviors. Thus, participants are asked to describe their *feelings* about the training activities and experiences and to rate training procedures as to how well they enjoyed doing them. This is not outcomes evaluation—unless, of course, the goal of the program is to have experiences that participants rate as pleasant and satisfying.

It is true, of course, that outcome-oriented short-term training programs do involve processes, and it is important to determine how students respond to these. We can often increase outcomes by improving process.

It is also possible to translate abstract goals of the type mentioned into observable, and thus somewhat measurable, behaviors. Increasing self-awareness, for example, might be measured by comparing self-estimates with actual performance and by the number of self-descriptive statements a participant can make before and after a training program.

However, if your sole purpose is for participants to have an experience that they rate as worthwhile, don't spend time trying to develop behavioral outcomes measures.

Our basic suggestion is simply to be as clear as you can regarding program goals and then use appropriate evaluation procedures. If your goal is increased performance, obtain measures of behavior and use these as a basis of evaluation. Don't evaluate the *effectiveness* of your training program on the basis of how students reacted to the process.

Participants' performance

Let's look at some issues regarding the measurement of performance. The simplest way to determine whether people have learned to perform a task is to observe them trying to do it. This works well with simple tasks. If you can thread a pipe or change a flat tire in a course, there is a very high probability that you can thread other pipes and change other tires under different circumstances. Thus, measuring performance can be done in the program.

However, as the subject matter becomes more complex and abstract, so does the task of measuring outcomes. We can no longer assume that a participant who can perform under one set of conditions will be able to do so under others. The problem with measuring the outcomes is that there are too many different conditions. To test performance under all of them would be impractical.

Consequently, we can observe only a sample of all possible situations. The trouble is we may not select an adequate sample.

For example, a student in a program designed to train cooks for a fast-food restaurant may perform adequately within the confines of the program. Even under simulated pressure of equipment breakdown and heavy orders, his performance holds up. On the job, however, he may experience such conditions as inadequate supervision, incompetent coworkers, and material shortages, any one of which may cause his performance to fall below requirements. The task in evaluation is to include the conditions that are most critical to on-the-job performance.

Another issue that complicates outcomes evaluation is skill or concept application. When a short-term training program is concerned with teaching skills or concepts that must be applied in a variety of situations, it is seldom possible to test participants in all those situations. That is, participants are expected to extend their abilities beyond those areas included in training. Participants learn how to prepare a summary of daily sales transactions, using a clothing store as a training example. Can they apply the skills involved when they are employed in other settings, such as a hardware store?

Predicting performance

The task of obtaining useful outcomes measures can be depicted by the following symbol: $B_1 \rightarrow B_2$. B_1 is the participant's behavior on our training test. B_2 is the participant's behavior under real job conditions. The measurement task is to choose B_1 (test) behaviors that adequately represent B_2 behaviors. We want, in other words, to be able to *predict* real performance (B_2) from test performance (B_1). In technical terms we need a valid test—one that does a good job of predicting B_2. There are several ways of increasing validity.

One is to have a clear understanding of the nature of the real performance requirements and conditions. Study the tasks carefully (which should be done during the design phase) and also examine the environmental situation. What conditions arise that could affect performance? What kinds of applications and generalizations may be required?

One way to view the performance environment is to use a classification system that identifies different kinds of performance outcomes. One useful classification is information, behavior, and attitudes. To identify these, examine the performance situation, asking the following questions:

What information, such as facts, rules, and policies, is required to perform adequately? What concepts are required?

What skills are necessary for adequate performance?

What attitudes are important for adequate performance?

You will recall from chapter 5 that the design phase we described includes listing these kinds of outcomes. When the design has been done carefully and identifies specific outcomes, a foundation for outcomes evaluation already exists. You select sample outcomes representing all three categories and then develop test items and tasks.

The use of such a procedure helps assure that all parts of the performance are included in your test and that each item in your test has a function. A common way of making up tests is to write a list of items that seem to be related to the instruction. What frequently happens is that items are included that have little or nothing to do with performance. Asking participants to name the author of the text, to tell who said what and when, and to recite formulas that will never be used doesn't tell you very much about the participants' ability to perform. To start by looking at the desired outcomes help avoid such items as these and zeros in on the important concerns of your instruction.

Another way of increasing the validity of your outcomes evaluation procedures is to make them as reliable as possible. Just as you wouldn't use an elastic ruler to measure length, you don't want to use an unreliable test to measure performance. When a test is reliable, it gives the same measure on a given individual each time it is applied, assuming that learning hasn't taken place in between. If, for example, a participant answers seventy-five out of one hundred questions correctly on Monday morning and only twenty-five of the same questions correctly on Monday afternoon, the test is probably not very reliable. There are ways of increasing test reliability. See references in chapter 9 for explanations of these.

Relative and absolute performance

It is very important to know why you are measuring outcomes. Most of us grew up when schools and other places that gave tests used a normative or comparative frame of reference. That is, an individual's test results were described in relation to how a group of people scored. An intelligence quotient (I.Q.), for example, compares you with all other people your age. And to say that Mary scored at the seventy-fifth percentile on the computer programming course exam is to compare Mary's score with all other students who took the course.

The practice of thinking of test scores in regard to the performance of a norm group can be misleading. We can only touch upon the problem here.

The alternative to using a normative frame of reference is to think in terms of absolute performance. Often referred to as "criterion referenced testing," the procedure involves establishing the lowest acceptable performance level (test score) and determining whether a given participant is below or above it. It matters little how far above or below, and how many in a class make the absolute score is usually not relevant. For measurement purposes, either you can do it or you can't. No almosts, sometimes, or maybes.

The trick, of course, is to determine the absolute minimal level of acceptable performance. How many times out of ten tries must a student completing a transcription course prepare perfect copy? It depends on the situation. Is it a record of court testimony upon which someone's life may depend? Or is it a thank-you note for a small business favor? Is the task operating a fire extinguisher on a 747 or making an accurate serve in tennis?

Whatever the case, if you can decide upon the absolute performance level required, there are advantages of economy and ease of measurement in using a criterion-based frame of reference.

For one thing, students can terminate training as soon as they demonstrate acceptable competency. This is quite a different situation from when competency is demonstrated by completing a course. For another, the complexity of designing measuring instruments is lessened.

To repeat, measuring outcomes indirectly via tests and sample performances is a complex undertaking. Instructor-made tests are notoriously unreliable and invalid. This is unfortunate because people's lives are often affected significantly by such attempts to measure outcomes. But that is no reason to avoid outcomes evaluation. Just the opposite. Because so many important decisions are based on results of training, it is critical that we become more skilled at obtaining outcomes measures.

9 Resources

In the previous eight chapters, we presented the basic framework of a model for short-term training. We've just touched the surface. There is, of course, much more to be said and many questions to be answered. Many of the questions begin with *How*: How do you make clear goal statements? How do you actually define program design specifications? How do you develop media materials? How can computers be used in short-term training? How do you actually solve climate-building problems? How do you do outcomes evaluation for specific subjects? The list of specific issues and questions regarding short-term training goes on and on.

This chapter points to initial answers to these kinds of questions. The annotated references that follow have been included because they are brief, to the point, and practical. Most of them also contain references to further resources.

DEVELOPING GOALS

Gronlund, Norman E. *Stating Objectives for Classroom Instruction.* 2d ed. New York: Macmillan Publishing Company, Inc., 1978.

"Intended as a practical guide on the preparation of instructional objectives for classroom teaching, testing, and evaluation." This 74-page booklet is useful. Its public school orientation does detract from substantive issues at times. Brief discussion of taxonomy of educational objectives, which considers cognitive, affective, and psychomotor objectives, will be enlightening to reader with minimal training in education.

Mager, Robert F. *Preparing Instructional Objectives.* 2d ed. Belmont, Calif.: Fearon-Pitman Publishers, Inc., 1975.

———. *Goal Analysis.* Belmont, Calif.: Fearon-Pitman Publishers, Inc., 1972.

These are two of several handbooks that Mager has written about designing instructional programs. His approach emphasizes being very clear about what it is you want people to learn. He does an excellent job of illustrating what he means. Well written, with many helpful examples of both clear and fuzzy objectives . . . pointing up how the latter can get you in trouble.

DESIGN AND TEACHING PROCEDURES

Dickinson, Gary. *Teaching Adults: A Handbook for Instructors.* Toronto: New Press, 1973.

This book is written for part-time instructors who have little or no knowledge of the principles of teaching and learning. The five chapter topics are the nature of adult learning, characteristics of the adult learner, principles of course planning, principles of instruction, and evaluation. Essentially, the author identifies basic learning principles derived from research and then develops suggestions and cautions based on these. It includes pre- and post-tests for each chapter and is written in a straightforward style.

McLagan, Patricia A. *Helping Others Learn: Designing Programs for Adults.* Reading, Mass.: Addison-Wesley Publishing Company, 1978.

The author defines learning as changes in knowledge, behavior, and values. This short book (101 pages) is divided into four sections: Motivation, Information Processing, Learning Results, and Application and Transfer. It provides a useful perspective for developing short-term training programs. The emphasis on individual differences is especially helpful.

Pfeiffer, J. William, and Jones, John E., eds. *The Annual Handbook for Group Facilitators*. LaJolla, Calif.: University Associates, 1972–79.

There is a totally new annual each year. They contain current, nonoverlapping collections of structured experiences, instruments, lecturettes, theory and practice papers, resources, bibliographies, and book reviews. Although they are specifically intended for trainers of human relations type courses, there are occasional items relevant to more general program design and development, and of course the structured exercises provide a fountain of ideas for climate-building procedures.

INSTRUCTIONAL TECHNOLOGY

Rufsvold, Margaret. *Guides to Educational Media*. 4th ed. Chicago: American Library Association, 1977.

Describes catalogs, indexes, lists, and reviewing services that systematically provide information about educational media. Deals only with United States materials. Excludes trade catalogs and promotional publications. Covers a wide range of content areas.

Taggart, Dorothy T. *A Guide to Sources in Educational Media and Technology*. Metuchen, New Jersey: The Scarecrow Press, Inc., 1975.

Written to "aid the librarian in finding the materials that he needs," this little volume is also a valuable resource for instructors. Especially useful annotated bibliographies covering uses of media. Topics include instructional film and television, facility planning, programmed instruction, system evaluation, professional organizations, periodicals, plus thirteen more. A good place to start if you want to explore the world of educational technology.

CLIMATE BUILDING

Pfeiffer, J. W., and Jones, J. E., eds. *A Handbook of Structured*

Experiences for Human Relations Training. vols. 1–5. La Jolla, Calif.: University Associates, 1973–75.

There are 122 structured experiences designed to promote varied learning outcomes. Of particular value for the short-term training staff are the ideas for climate building—getting acquainted exercises and contract building ideas. There is a continuing series, so ensure that you get on University Associates' mailing list:

> University Associates, Inc.
> 7596 Eads Avenue
> La Jolla, California 92037

Thayer, Louis, ed. *Affective Education: Strategies for Experiential Learning.* La Jolla, Calif.: University Associates, 1976.

Designed to be applicable in a wide range of educational-learning settings and subject matter areas, the fifty structured exercises seek to strengthen the affective components of learning—the learners' self-awareness, learning climates, interpersonal relationships in learning, recognition of learner needs and perceptions, and skills required for facilitating learning. A good application of experiential learning techniques.

EVALUATION

Gronlund, Norman E. *Preparing Criterion-Referenced Tests for Classroom Instruction.* New York: Macmillan Publishing Company, Inc., 1973.

A practical beginning guide for preparing criterion-referenced tests. Our chapter 8 referred to these as absolute measures of achievement. Includes suggestions for true-false and matching items as well as multiple-choice items. Gives examples of planning for tests. Public school orientation can be annoying but not significantly distracting.

Mager, Robert F. *Measuring Instructional Intent, or Got a Match?* Belmont, Calif.: Lear Siegler, Inc./Fearon-Pitman Publishers, Inc., 1973.

A popularized approach to developing objective tests. This book is clearly written with sharp examples and self-testing features. It lays out a method of developing achievement measures, which if followed will probably improve your tests.

Townsend, Arthur, and Burke, Paul J. *Using Statistics in Classroom Instruction.* New York: Macmillan Publishing Company, Inc., 1975.

Straightforward description of statistics necessary for outcomes evaluation. The statistics included can be done on inexpensive hand calculators much more rapidly than by the formulas given in the book. The value of the book is in clarifying the nature of these basic statistics.

GENERAL

Argus Communications, 7440 Natchez Avenue, Niles, Illinois 60648.

This organization produces a wide range of beautifully designed inexpensive posters, which we use widely in our courses. They range from funny, cynical, and uplifting to thought-provoking. Get their catalog.

Craig, Robert, ed. *Training and Development Handbook, A Guide to Human Resource Development.* 2d ed. New York: McGraw-Hill, 1977.

Contains forty-nine chapters written by authorities in various aspects of training. Recommended by American Society for Training and Development as a basic reference for trainers.

Davis, Larry N. *Planning, Conducting, Evaluating Workshops.* Austin, Texas: Learning Concepts, 1975.

With the exception of this book, the only other general text that is geared primarily to short-term training. Many practical tips on planning workshops—assigning needs, specifying objectives, designing learning activities, budgeting, and making arrangements. There are also valuable guides to conducting and evaluating workshops within the context of adult education. There are many useful checklists.

Knowles, Malcolm S. *Self-directed Learning: A Guide for Learners and Teachers.* Chicago: Association Press/Follett Publishing Company, 1975.

Knowles states that " 'self-directed learning' describes a process in which individuals take the initiative, with or without the help of others, in diagnosing their learning needs, formulating learning goals, identifying human and material resources for learning, choosing and implementing appropriate learning strategies, and evaluating learning outcomes." In this brief book of 135 pages, Knowles illustrates how instructors can facilitate this process. Very practical, full of concrete examples.

Training and Development Journal. American Society for Training and Development.

The ASTD is a national professional organization for trainers. In addition to this monthly journal, it publishes and distributes films, resource directories, and a variety of other instructional materials. It also conducts seminars and holds an annual conference. For information regarding materials and membership, write to:

> American Society for Training and Development
> P. O. Box 5307
> Madison, Wisconsin 53705

Glossary

Block design Participants will be together for a continuous period of time.

Climate The psychological and social atmosphere of a course.

Closed course Participants must be there at the beginning and stay until the end.

Conducting Actually running the course from the moment the first participant arrives until the moment the last one leaves.

Context profile A list of all possible environmental factors to be considered when planning a program.

Contracting Always involves three phases: (1) between trainers and contractor, (2) between contractor and participants, (3) between trainers and participants.

Contractor The person who provides the budget for and underwrites the program.

Designing Describing what the program should accomplish and how. It is akin to a blueprint for the course.

Developing Making the blueprint happen. Developing teaching materials, planning, making arrangements for equipment and facilities, rehearsing instructional procedures, checking the program for possible deterrents to climate, and making administrative arrangements.

Evaluating Making judgments about the effectiveness of the training, using preordained criteria both during and after the course.

External trainers Consultants or others who are not part of the organizations from which the participants come.

In-house training Programs designed for working within an organization with participants who probably know one another to some extent and who may even work together.

Instructor   A trainer.

Instructor credibility   Ability of trainer to gain respect and trust of participants.

Internal trainers   Consultants or others who are part of the organizations from which participants come.

Lightener   An activity that is pertinent to the teaching objectives but whose primary function is helping participants relax, laugh, and have a good time.

Low error tolerance   Small capacity for errors or redirection (program).

Norms   The stated and unstated values and attitudes that guide the behavior of groups and organization.

One-shot design   A course that is specially designed and may never be used again.

Ongoing assessment   Monitoring the reactions of participants as the course proceeds.

Open course   Participants can join or leave the course at different stages.

Pacing   Timing a presentation or series of teaching procedures.

Participants   Students or trainees. In general, participants in short-term training programs are less put off from staff than students in traditional instruction.

Residential course   Course whose participants live in—stay on the premises overnight.

Serial design   Participants will be brought together for more than one block of time—one evening a week, two weekends, and so on.

Short-term training   Our arbitrary definition requires that (1) it take place within a period of one hour to three or four weeks; (2) it be a response to specific requests or problems; (3) it not be part of scheduled ongoing recurring instruction; and (4) both instructor and students be aware of the intensity involved.

Staff   Trainers plus all other nonparticipants involved in producing a program.

Teaching procedures   The technique of teaching to be used (e.g., presentation, demonstration, group learning, individual learning, structured experiences).

Teaching structures   The physical groupings of staff and participants (e.g., total group, in pairs, buzz groups, fishbowl).

"Thinking on your feet"   Reacting quickly to ongoing developments in the course. It involves being able to monitor participants' reactions sensitively and having alternative strategies and inputs to offer.

Trainer   A person who presents, explains, demonstrates, facilitates, or otherwise contributes directly to the learning of participants in training programs.

Warm-up activities   Helping people break the ice and get involved *and* committed to the course.

Index